A Stone, A Leaf, A Door

A Stone, A Leaf, A Door

POEMS

BY THOMAS WOLFE

Selected and Arranged in Verse by

JOHN S. BARNES

With a Foreword by
LOUIS UNTERMEYER

New York
CHARLES SCRIBNER'S SONS

Foreword

By Louis Untermeyer

It has often been suggested that Thomas Wolfe was a poet who elected to write in prose. This volume proves the suggestion to be a fact. More than anything else, Wolfe wanted to be a poet. But, as John Hall Wheelock discloses in his Introduction to *The Face of a Nation*, Wolfe placed so much emphasis on conventional form that he confused the shape with the spirit of his hugely sprawling lines and cast himself out of the company of poets.

Now Sergeant J. S. Barnes has gone over everything Wolfe ever wrote, and he has discovered that most of the writing is not only rhapsodic—a discovery likely to be made by the casual reader—but that much of it falls into deeply rhythmical, strongly cadenced verse. Re-arranging or, rather, re-spacing the long plunging passages, he has broken down the line between prose and verse. Revealing the pure poetic impetus which propels *Look Homeward, Angel* and *Of Time and the River*, and is even more compelling in the later work, this selection restores Wolfe to the company from which he fearfully excluded himself and to which he rightfully belongs.

It may be objected that the editor tries to make Wolfe a poet by manipulation, by a mere typographical trick. But the rearrangement is neither arbitrary nor whimsical; it is implicit in Wolfe's language, logical in the rise and fall of the sentences, in the ebb and flow which reflect the tidal emotions. In no prose and only in a small body of verse has there been expressed a greater sense of American life: its range and richness, its vast pride and intemperate gusto, its unhappy adolescent yearnings and insatiable appetite. Here, in these illuminating pages, are concentrated the extremes of ecstasy and disillusion, of love and cruelty, the wandering passions of the human spirit. The mood shifts from agonized doubt to quiet affirmation, from the lyrical contemplation of a plum-tree to the mystical evocation of black night "with all its lonely wilderness of storm . . . striding like an enemy." Here are the light fantasies and echoes of forgotten time ("Play Us a Tune"), and here are the elemental questions which disturb the most untroubled life:

Which of us has known his brother?
Which of us has looked into his father's heart?
Which of us has not remained forever prison-pent?
Which of us is not forever a stranger and alone?

Here, rising from the narrative of *You Can't Go Home Again,* is that powerful soliloquy "This is Man," a profound monologue, beginning in devastating pessimism and ending in sheer exaltation.

Those readers who are already acquainted with Wolfe will recognize an aspect which they suspected but never wholly realized. Those who are not intimately acquainted with the novelist will discover a new American poet.

Contents

A Stone, A Leaf, A Door

. . . A stone, a leaf, an unfound door;
Of a stone, a leaf, a door.
And of all the forgotten faces.

Naked and alone we came into exile.
In her dark womb
We did not know our mother's face;
From the prison of her flesh have we come
Into the unspeakable and incommunicable prison
Of this earth.

Which of us has known his brother?
Which of us has looked into his father's heart?
Which of us has not remained forever prison-pent?
Which of us is not forever a stranger and alone?

O waste of loss, in the hot mazes, lost,
Among bright stars
On this most weary unbright cinder, lost!
Remembering speechlessly
We seek the great forgotten language,
The lost lane-end into heaven,
A stone, a leaf, an unfound door.

Ben

My Brother Ben's face, thought Eugene,
Is like a piece of slightly yellow ivory;
His high white head is knotted fiercely
By his old man's scowl;
His mouth is like a knife,
His smile the flicker of light across a blade.
His face is like a blade, and a knife,
And a flicker of light:
It is delicate and fierce,
And scowls beautifully forever,
And when he fastens his hard white fingers
And his scowling eyes
Upon a thing he wants to fix,
He sniffs
With sharp and private concentration
Through his long pointed nose.
Thus women, looking, feel a well of tenderness
For his pointed, bumpy, always scowling face:
His hair shines like that of a young boy—
It is crinkled and crisp as lettuce.

Yesterday, Remember?

Strange aerial music
Came fluting out of darkness,

Or over his slow-wakening senses
Swept the great waves
Of symphonic orchestration.
Fiend-voices, beautiful and sleep-loud,
Called down through darkness and light,
Developing the thread of ancient memory.

Staggering blindly in the whitewashed glare,
His eyes, sleep-corded, opened slowly
As he was born anew,
Umbilically cut,
From darkness.

Waken, ghost-eared boy,
But into darkness.
Waken, phantom, O into us.
Try, try, O try the way.
Open the wall of light.

Ghost, ghost,
Who is the ghost?
O lost.
Ghost, ghost,
Who is the ghost?

O whisper-tongued laughter.
Eugene! Eugene!
Here, O here, Eugene.

Here, Eugene.
The way is here, Eugene.
Have you forgotten?

The leaf, the rock, the wall of light.
Lift up the rock, Eugene,
The leaf, the stone, the unfound door.
Return, return.

A voice, sleep-strange and loud,
Forever far-near,
Spoke.

Eugene!

Spoke, ceased,
Continued without speaking, to speak.
In him spoke.

Where darkness, soon, is light.
Try, boy, the word you know remember.
In the beginning was the logos.
Over the border the borderless green-forested land.
Yesterday, remember?

Far-forested, a horn-note wound.
Sea-forested, water-far,
The grotted coral sea-far horn-note.

The pillioned ladies
Witch-faced in bottle-green robes
Saddle-swinging.
Merwomen unscaled and lovely
In sea-floor colonnades.

The hidden land below the rock.
The flitting wood-girls
Growing into bark.
Far-faint, as he wakened,
They besought him with lessening whir.
Then deeper song, fiend-throated, wind-shod.

Brother, O brother!

They shot down the brink of darkness,
Gone on the wind like bullets.

O Lost

We shall not come again.
We never shall come back again.
But over us all, over us all,
Over us all is—something.

Wind pressed the boughs;
The withered leaves were shaking.

It was October, but some leaves were shaking.

A light swings over the hill.
(We shall not come again.)
And over the town a star.
(Over us all, over us all that shall not come again.)
And over the day the dark.
But over the darkness—
What?

We shall not come again.
We never shall come back again.

Over the dawn a lark. (That shall not come again.)
And wind and music far.
O lost! (It shall not come again.)
And over your mouth the earth.
O ghost!
But, over the darkness—
What?

Wind pressed the boughs;
The withered leaves were quaking.

We shall not come again.
We never shall come back again.
It was October,
But we never shall come back again.

When will they come again?
When will they come again?

The laurel, the lizard, and the stone
Will come no more.
The women weeping at the gate have gone,
And will not come again.
And pain and pride and death will pass,
And will not come again.
And light and dawn will pass,
And the star and the cry of a lark will pass,
And will not come again.
And we shall pass,
And shall not come again.

What things will come again?
Oh, Spring, the cruellest and fairest of the seasons,
Will come again.
And the strange and buried men
Will come again,
In flower and leaf
The strange and buried men
Will come again,
And death and the dust will never come again,
For death and the dust
Will die.

And Ben will come again,

He will not die again,
In flower and leaf,
In wind and music far,
He will come back again.

O lost,
And by the wind grieved,
Ghost,
Come back again.

Artemidorus, Farewell!

We can believe in the nothingness of life,
We can believe in the nothingness of death
And of life after death—
But who can believe in the nothingness of Ben?

Like Apollo,
Who did his penance to the high god
In the sad house of King Admetus,
He came,
A god with broken feet,
Into the gray hovel of this world.

He lived here a stranger,
Trying to recapture the music
Of the lost world,
Trying to recall

The great forgotten language,
The lost faces,
The stone, the leaf, the door.

O Artemidorus, farewell!

Royal Processional

And Eugene watched the slow fusion
Of the seasons;
He saw the royal processional
Of the months;
He saw the summer light
Eat like a river into dark;
He saw dark triumph once again;
And he saw the minute-winning days,
Like flies,
Buzz home to death.

In summer,
Full day had come before he finished:
He walked home in a world of wakenings.
The first cars were grouped on the Square
As he passed,
Their new green paint giving them
The pleasant appearance of fresh toys.
The huge battered cans of the milkmen

Glinted cleanly in the sun.
Light fell hopefully
Upon the swarthy greasiness of George Chakales,
Nightman of the Athens Café.
The Hellenic Dawn.

And in Uneeda No. 1, upon the Square,
Eugene sat,
Washing an egg-sandwich down
With long swallows of pungent coffee,
Stooled in a friendly company
Of motormen, policemen,
Chauffeurs, plasterers, and masons.
It was very pleasant, he felt,
To complete one's work
When all the world was beginning theirs.
He went home under singing trees of birds.

In autumn,
A late red moon rode low in the skies
Till morning.
The air was filled with dropping leaves,
There was a solemn thunder
Of great trees upon the hills;
Sad phantasmal whisperings
And the vast cathedral music
Deepened in his heart.

In winter,
He went down joyously into the dark howling wind,
Leaning his weight upon its advancing wall
As it swept up a hill;

And when in early Spring
The small cold rain
Fell from the reeking sky
He was content.
He was alone.

Magic

And who shall say—
Whatever disenchantment follows—
That we ever forget magic,
Or that we can ever betray,
On this leaden earth,
The apple-tree, the singing,
And the gold?

Niggertown

Below him in the valley,
Across on the butte,
The smoky lamps of Niggertown
Flared in the dusk.

Faint laughter, rich, jungle-wild,
Welled up from hived darkness.
He heard lost twangling notes,
The measured thump
Of distant feet.

Beyond, above,
More thin,
More far than all,
The rapid wail of sinners
In a church.

Gant

In the cool long glade of yard
That stretched four hundred feet behind the house
He planted trees and grape vines.
And whatever he touched
In that rich fortress of his soul
Sprang into golden life:
As the years passed, the fruit trees—
The peach, the plum, the cherry, the apple—
Grew great and bent beneath their clusters.

His grape vines thickened
Into brawny ropes of brown
And coiled down the high wire fences of his lot,
And hung in a dense fabric, upon his trellises,

Roping his domain twice around.
They climbed the porch end of the house
And framed the upper windows in thick bowers.

And the flowers grew in rioting glory in his yard—
The velvet-leaved nasturtium,
Slashed with a hundred tawny dyes,
The rose, the snowball,
The red-cupped tulip, and the lily.
The honeysuckle drooped its heavy mass
Upon the fence;
Wherever his great hands touched the earth
It grew fruitful for him.

Eugene

And left alone
To sleep within a shuttered room,
With the thick sunlight
Printed in bars upon the floor,
Unfathomable loneliness and sadness
Crept through him:
He saw his life
Down the solemn vista of a forest aisle,
And he knew he would always be the sad one:
Caged in that little round of skull,
Imprisoned in that beating and most secret heart,
His life must always walk

Down lonely passages.
Lost.

He understood
That men were forever strangers
To one another,
That no one ever comes really
To know another,
That, imprisoned in the dark womb
Of our mother,
We come to life
Without having seen her face,
That we are given to her arms
A stranger,
And that, caught
In that insoluble prison of being,
We escape it never,
No matter what arms may clasp us,
What mouth may kiss us,
What heart may warm us.
Never, never, never, never, never.

Dance

But they danced there slowly
In a gray light of dusk
That was like pain and beauty;
Like the lost light undersea,

In which his life, a lost merman,
Swam, remembering exile.

And as they danced
She, whom he dared not touch,
Yielded her body unto him,
Whispering softly to his ear,
Pressing with slender fingers
His hot hand.

And she, whom he would not touch,
Lay there, like a sheaf of grain,
In the crook of his arm,
Token of the world's remedy—
The refuge from the one lost face
Out of all the faces,
The anodyne against the wound named Laura—
A thousand flitting shapes of beauty
To bring him comfort and delight.

The great pageantry of pain and pride and death
Hung through the dusk its awful vision,
Touching his sorrow with a lonely joy.
He had lost;
But all pilgrimage across the world was loss:
A moment of cleaving, a moment of taking away,
The thousand phantom shapes that beaconed,
And the high impassionate grief of stars.

The Cock That Crows at Morning

Wind pressed the boughs.
It was still dark.
But above them the thick clouds
That had covered the earth for days
With a dreary gray blanket
Had been torn open.

Eugene looked up
Through the deep ragged vault
Of the sky
And saw the proud and splendid stars,
Bright and unwinking.
The withered leaves were shaking.
A cock crew his shrill morning cry
Of life beginning and awakening.

The cock that crew at midnight,
Thought Eugene,
Had an elfin ghostly cry.
His crow was drugged with sleep
And death:
It was like a far horn
Sounding under sea;
And it was a warning to all the men

Who are about to die,
And to the ghosts that must go home.

But the cock that crows at morning,
He thought,
Has a voice as shrill as any fife.
It says, we are done with sleep,
We are done with death.
Oh, waken, waken into life,
Says his voice
As shrill as any fife.

In that enormous silence,
Birds were waking.
He heard the cock's bright minstrelsy
Again,
And by the river in the dark,
The great thunder of flanged wheels,
And the long retreating wail of the whistle.
And slowly, up the chill deserted street,
He heard the heavy ringing clangour
Of shod hoofs.
In that enormous silence,
Life was waking.

Joy awoke in him, and exultation.
They had escaped from the prison
Of death;

They were joined to the bright engine of life
Again.
Life, ruddered life, that would not fail,
Began its myriad embarkations.

Play Us a Tune

Play us a tune on an unbroken spinet,
And let the bells ring,
Let the bells ring!
Play music now:
Play us a tune on an unbroken spinet.

Do not make echoes of forgotten time,
Do not strike music from old broken keys,
Do not make ghosts
With faded tinklings on the yellowed board;
But play us a tune on an unbroken spinet,
Play lively music
When the instrument was new,
Let us see Mozart playing in the parlor,
And let us hear the sound of the ladies' voices.

But more than that;
Waken the turmoil of forgotten streets,
Let us hear their sound again,
Unmuted, and unchanged by time,

Throw the light of Wednesday morning
On the Third Crusade,
And let us see Athens on an average day.
Let us hear the sound of the voices of the Greeks,
And observe closely if they were all wise and beautiful
At ten o'clock in the morning;
Let us see if their limbs were all perfect,
And their gestures grave and stately,
Also let us smell their food and observe them eating,
And hear, if only once,
The sound of a wheel in a street,
The texture of just four forgotten moments.

Give us the sounds of Egypt on a certain day;
Let us hear the voice of King Menkaura
And some of the words of the Lady Sennuwy;
Also the voices of the cotton-farmers.
Let us hear the vast and casual sound of life,
In these old peoples:
Their greetings in the street,
The voices of the housewives and the merchants.
And let us hear the laughter of a woman
In the sixteenth century.

The cry of the wolf would always be the same;
The sound of the wheel will always be the same;
And the hoof of the horse
On the roads of every time will be the same.

But play us a tune on an unbroken spinet;
And let us hear the voices of knights at dinner.

The cry of a man to his dog,
And the barking of the dog;
The call of the plow-driver to his horse,
And the sound of the horse;
The noise of the hunt,
And the sound of the flowing water,
Will always be the same.

By the waters of life,
By time, by time,
Play us a tune on an unbroken spinet,
And let us hear the actual voices of old fairs;
Let us move backward through our memories,
And through the memory of the race,
Let us relive
The million forgotten moments of our lives,
And let us see poor people
Sitting in their rooms in 1597,
And let us see the rich man
Standing with his back before the fire,
In the Middle Ages,
And his wife knitting by the table,
And let us hear their casual words.

Let us see the men

Who built the houses of Old Frankfort;
Let us see how they worked,
And let us see them
Sitting on hewn timbers when they ate their lunches;
Let us hear their words,
The sound of their voices.

Unwind the fabric of lost time
Out of our entrails,
Repair the million little threads of actual circumstance
Until the seconds grow gray, bright and dusty
With the living light,
And we see the plain unfabled faces of the people;
Let us awake, and hear the people in the streets,
And see Tobias Smollett pass our window.

Then, play us a tune on the unbroken spinet,
Let time be as the road to London
And we a traveller on it;
And let us enter London
And find out what year it is there in the Mile End Road;
Let it be dark, and let us enter London in the dark,
And hear men's voices,
And let us see if we could understand them;
And let us then find out what year it is,
A lodging for the night,
And see if they read mystery on us,
Or would fly away from us.

Father, I Know That You Live

By the waters of life,
Before we knew that we must die,
Before we had seen our father's face,
Before we had sought the print of his foot:
By the waters of time
(The tide! the tide!),
Before we had seen the shadows in the haunted woods,
Before lost moments lived again,
Before the shades were fleshed.

Who are we,
That must follow in the footsteps of the king?
Who are we,
That had no kings to follow?
We are the unkinged men.
Have we left shadows on forgotten walls?
Have we crossed running water
And lived for seven timeless years with the enchantress,
And shall we find our son who is ourself,
And will he know us?

Shall your voices unlock the gates of my brain?
Shall I know you,
Though I have never seen your face?
Will you know me,
And will you call me "son"?

Father, I know that you live,.
Though I have never found you.

Yuh Musta Been Away

For suddenly you remember
How the tragic light of evening falls
Even on the huge and rusty jungle of the earth
That is known as Brooklyn
And on the faces of all the men
With dead eyes and with flesh of tallow gray,
And of how even in Brooklyn
They lean upon the sills of evening
In that sad hushed light.

And you remember
How you lay one evening on your couch
In your cool cellar depth in Brooklyn,
And listened to the sounds of evening
And to the dying birdsong in your tree;
And you remember how two windows were thrown up,
And you heard two voices—
A woman's and a man's—
Begin to speak in that soft tragic light.
And the memory of their words came back to you,
Like the haunting refrain of some old song—
As it was heard and lost in Brooklyn.

"Yuh musta been away," said one, in that sad light.
"Yeah, I been away. I just got back," the other said.
"Yeah? Dat's just what I was t'inkin'," said the other.
　　　"I'd been t'inkin' dat you musta been away."
"Yeah, I been away on my vacation. I just got back."
"Oh, yeah? Dat's what I t'ought meself.
　　　I was t'inkin' just duh oddeh day
　　　Dat I hadn't seen yuh f'r some time,
　　　'I guess she's gone away,' I says."

And then for seconds there was silence—
Save for the dying birdsong,
Voices in the street,
Faint sounds and shouts and broken calls,
And something hushed in evening,
Far, immense, murmurous in the air.

"Well, wat's t' noos sinct I been gone?"
The voice went out in quietness in soft soft tragic light.
"Has anyt'ing happened sinct I was away?"

"Nah! Nuttins happened," the other made reply.
"About duh same as usual—*you* know?" it said
With difficult constraint,
Inviting intuitions for the spare painfulness of barren
　　　tongues.

"Yeah, I know," the other answered

With a tranquil resignation—
And there was silence then in Brooklyn.

"I guess Fatheh Grogan died sinct you was gone,"
A voice began.
"Oh, yeah?" the other voice replied
With tranquil interest.
"Yeah."
And for a waiting moment there was silence.

"Say, dat's too bad, isn't it?"
The quiet voice then said
With comfortless regret.
"Yeah. He died on Sattiday.
        When he went home on Friday night,
        He was O.K."
"Oh, yeah?"
"Yeah."
And for a moment they were balanced in strong silence.

"Gee, dat was tough, wasn't it?"
"Yeah. Dey didn't find him
        Till duh next day at ten o'clock.
        When dey went to look for him
        He was lyin' stretched out
        On duh bat' room floeh."
"Oh, yeah?"
"Yeah. Dey found him lyin' deh," it said.

And for a moment more the voices hung in balanced
    silence.

"Gee, dat's too bad. . . .
      I guess I was away
      When all dat happened."
"Yeah. Yuh musta been away."
"Yeah, dat was it, I guess.
      I musta been away.
      Oddehwise I woulda hoid.
      I was away."

"Well, so long, kid. . . . I'll be seein' yuh."
"Well, so long!"

A window closed, and there was silence;
Evening and far sounds and broken cries in Brooklyn,
Brooklyn,
In the formless, rusty, and unnumbered wilderness of
    life.

And now the red light fades swiftly
From the old red brick of rusty houses,
And there are voices in the air,
And somewhere music,
And we are lying there,
Blind atoms in our cellar-depths,
Gray voiceless atoms

In the manswarm desolation of the earth,
And our fame is lost, our names forgotten,
Our powers are wasting from us like mined earth,
While we lie here at evening and the river flows . . .
And dark time is feeding like a vulture on our entrails,
And we know that we are lost, and cannot stir . . .
And there are ships there!
There are ships!
And Christ! We are all dying in the darkness! . . .

And yuh musta been away . . . yuh musta been
     away . . .

In Silence

Was it not well to leave all things as he had found
     them,
In silence, at the end?
Might it not be that in this great dream of time
In which we live and are the moving figures
There is no greater certitude than this:
That, having met, spoken,
Known each other for a moment,
As somewhere on this earth we were hurled onward
Through the darkness between two points of time,
It is well to be content with this,
To leave each other as we met,

Letting each one go alone to his appointed destination,
Sure of this only, needing only this—
That there will be silence for us all
And silence only,
Nothing but silence,
At the end?

Like the River

Why are you absent in the night, my love?
Where are you when the bells ring in the night?
Now, there are bells again,
How strange to hear the bells
In this vast, sleeping city!
Now, in a million little towns,
Now in the dark and lonely places of this earth,
Small bells are ringing out the time!
O my dark soul,
My child, my darling, my beloved,
Where are you now,
And in what place,
And in what time?
Oh, ring, sweet bells, above him
While he sleeps!
I send my love to you upon those bells.

Strange time, forever lost,
Forever flowing like the river!

Lost time, lost people, and lost love—
Forever lost!
There's nothing you can hold
There in the river!
There's nothing you can keep
There in the river!
It takes your love, it takes your life,
It takes the great ships going out to sea,
And it takes time,
Dark, delicate time,
The little ticking moments of strange time
That count us into death.

Now in the dark
I hear the passing of dark time,
And all the sad and secret flowing of my life.
All of my thoughts are flowing like the river,
All of my life is passing like the river,
I dream and talk and feel just like the river,
As it flows by me,
By me, to the sea.

The Way Things Are

This is the way things are.
Here is the grass,
So green and coarse, so sweet and delicate,

But with some brown rubble in it.

There are the houses all along the street,
The concrete blocks of walls,
Somehow so dreary,
Ugly, yet familiar,
The slate roofs and the shingles,
The lawns, the hedges and the gables,
The backyards with their accidental structures
Of so many little and familiar things
As hen houses, barns.

All common and familiar as my breath,
All accidental as the strings of blind chance,
Yet all somehow fore-ordered as a destiny:
The way they are,
Because
They are the way they are!

Pity

Pity, more than any other feeling,
Is a "learned" emotion;
A child will have it least of all.
Pity comes
From the infinite accumulations of man's memory,
From the anguish, pain, and suffering of life,
From the full deposit of experience,

From the forgotten faces, the lost men,
And from the million strange and haunting visages
Of time.

Pity comes upon the nick of time
And stabs us like a knife.
Its face is thin and dark and burning,
And it has come before we know it,
Gone before we can grasp or capture it;
It leaves a shrewd, deep wound,
But a bitter, subtle one,
And it always comes most keenly
From a little thing.

It comes, without a herald or a cause we can determine,
At some moment of our lives when we are
Far and lost from all the scenes that pity comes from;
And how, why, where it comes
We cannot say.
But suddenly in the city—
In the great and million-footed city—
Pity comes to us at evening
When the dust and fury of another city day is over,
And we lean upon the sills of evening
In an ancient life.

Then pity comes to us;
We will remember children's voices of long ago,

The free, full shout of sudden, gleeful laughter
From a child that we once knew,
Full of exulting innocence,
The songs that we sang on summer porches long ago,
A note of pride in our mother's voice
And her grave, worn eyes of innocence
As she boasted of a little thing,
The simple words that a woman we once loved had said
In some forgotten moment
When she left us for another day.

Then pity is there, is there at once
With its dark face and sudden knife,
To stab us with an anguish that we cannot utter,
To rend us with its agony
Of intolerable and wordless regret,
To haunt us with the briefness of our days,
And to tear our hearts with anguish and wild sorrow.

And for what? For what?
For all we want, that never may be captured,
For all we thirst for, that never may be found,
For love, that must grow old and be forever dying,
For all the bone, brain, passion, marrow, sinew
Of our lives, our hearts, our youth,
That must grow old and bowed and barren,
Wearied out!

And oh! for beauty,
That wild, strange song of magic, aching beauty,
The intolerable, unutterable, ungraspable
Glory, power, and beauty of this world,
This earth, this life, that is,
And is everywhere around us,
That we have seen and known
At ten thousand moments of our lives,
That has broken our hearts, maddened our brains,
And torn the sinews of our lives asunder
As we have lashed and driven savagely
Down the kaleidoscopic fury of the years
In quest of it,
Unresting in our frenzied hope
That some day we shall find it, hold it, fix it,
Make it ours forever—
And that now haunts us strangely, sorrowfully,
With its wild song and aching ecstasy
As we lean upon the sills of evening in the city.

We feel the sorrow and the hush
Of evening in the city,
The voices, quiet, casual, lonely,
Of the people,
Far cries and broken sounds,
And smell the sea, the harbor,
And the huge, slow breathing of deserted docks,
And know that there are ships there!

And beauty swells
Like a wild song in our heart,
Beauty bursting like a great grape in our throat,
Beauty aching, rending, wordless, and unutterable,
Beauty in us, all around us,
Never to be captured—
And we know that we are dying
As the river flows!

Oh, then will pity come,
Strange, sudden pity
With its shrewd knife and the asp of time
To stab us
With a thousand wordless, lost, forgotten,
Little things!

And how, where, why it came
We cannot say,
But we feel pity now
For all men who have ever lived upon the earth,
And it is night, now,
Night, and the great stars are flashing in the lilac dark,
The great stars are flashing
On a hundred million men across America,
And it is night, now,
Night, and we are living, hoping, fearing,
Loving, dying in the darkness,
While the great stars shine upon us

As they have shone on all men dead and living
On this earth,
On all men yet unborn, and yet to live
Who will come after us!

Night

The wasting helve of the moon rode into heaven
Over the bulk of the hills.
There was a smell of wet grass and lilac,
And the vast brooding symphony
Of the million-noted little night things,
Rising and falling in a constant ululation,
And inhabiting the heart
With steady unconscious certitude.

The pallid light drowned out the stars,
It lay like silence on the earth,
It dripped through the leafy web
Of the young maples,
Printing the earth with swarming moths
Of elvish light.

Death, Loneliness, and Sleep

Therefore, immortal fellowship,
Proud Death, stern Loneliness, and Sleep,

Dear friends, in whose communion I shall live forever,
Out of the passion and substance of my life
I have made this praise for you:

To you, proud Death, who sit so grandly
On the brows of little men—
First to you!
Proud Death, proud Death,
Whom I have seen by darkness,
At so many times,
And always when you came to nameless men!
What have you ever touched
That you have not touched with love and pity, Death?
Proud Death, wherever we have seen your face,
You came with mercy, love, and pity, Death,
And brought to all of us
Your compassionate sentences of pardon and release.

For have you not retrieved from exile
The desperate lives of men who never found their
        home?
Have you not opened your dark door
For us who never yet found doors to enter,
And given us a room
Who, roomless, doorless, unassuaged,
Were driven on forever through the streets of life?
Have you not offered us your stern provender, Death,
With which to stay the hunger

That grew to madness from the food it fed upon,
And given all of us the goal
For which we sought but never found,
The certitude, the peace,
For which our over-laden hearts contended,
And made for us, in your dark house,
An end of all the tortured wandering and unrest
That lashed us on forever?

Proud Death, proud Death,
Not for the glory that you added to the glory of the
     king,
Proud Death,
Nor for the honor you imposed upon the dignities of
     famous men,
Proud Death,
Nor for the final magic you have given to the lips of
     genius,
Death,
But because you come so gloriously to us
Who never yet knew glory,
So proudly and sublimely to us
Whose lives were nameless and obscure,
Because you give to all of us—
The nameless, faceless, voiceless atoms of the earth—
The awful chrysm of your grandeur,
Death,
Because I have seen and known you so well,

And have lived alone so long with Loneliness, your
     brother,
I do not fear you any longer, friend,
And I have made this praise for you.

Now Loneliness forever and the earth again!
Dark brother and stern friend,
Immortal face of darkness and of night,
With whom the half part of my life was spent,
And with whom I shall abide now till my death forever,
What is there for me to fear
As long as you are with me?

Heroic friend, blood-brother of proud Death,
Dark face,
Have we not gone together down a million streets,
Have we not coursed together the great and furious
     avenues of night,
Have we not crossed the stormy seas alone,
And known strange lands,
And come again to walk the continent of night,
And listen to the silence of the earth?
Have we not been brave and glorious when we were
     together,
Friend,
Have we not known triumph, joy, and glory on this
     earth—
And will it not be again with me

As it was then,
If you come back to me?

Come to me, brother, in the watches of the night,
Come to me in the secret and most silent heart of dark-
        ness,
Come to me as you always came,
Bringing to me once more
The old invincible strength, the deathless hope,
The triumphant joy and confidence
That will storm the ramparts of the earth again.

Come to me through the fields of night, dear friend,
Come to me with the horses of your sister, Sleep,
And we shall listen to the silence of the earth and dark-
        ness
Once again,
We shall listen to the heartbeats of the sleeping men,
As with soft and rushing thunder of their hooves
The strange dark horses of great Sleep come on again.

They come! Ships call!
The hooves of night, the horses of great Sleep,
Are coming on below their manes of darkness.
And forever the rivers run.
Deep as the tides of Sleep
The rivers run.
We call!

They come, my great dark horses come!
With soft and rushing thunder of their hooves they come,
And the horses of Sleep are galloping,
Galloping over the land.
Oh, softly, softly
The great dark horses of Sleep are galloping over the
    land.
The great black bats are flying over us.
The tides of Sleep are moving through the nation;
Beneath the tides of Sleep and time
Strange fish are moving.

For Sleep has crossed the worn visages of day,
And in the night-time, in the dark,
In all the sleeping silence of the towns,
The faces of ten million men are strange and dark as
    time.
In Sleep we lie all naked and alone,
In Sleep we are united at the heart of night and dark-
    ness,
And we are strange and beautiful asleep;
For we are dying in the darkness,
And we know no death, there is no death,
There is no life, no joy, no sorrow and no glory on
    the earth
But Sleep.

Come, mild and magnificent Sleep,

And let your tides flow through the nation.
O daughter of unmemoried desire, sister of Death,
And my stern comrade, Loneliness,
Bringer of peace and dark forgetfulness,
Healer and redeemer, dear enchantress,
Hear us:
Come to us through the fields of night,
Over the plains and rivers of the everlasting earth,
Bringing to the huge vexed substance of this world
And to all the fury, pain, and madness of our lives
The merciful anodyne of your redemption.
Seal up the porches of our memory,
Tenderly, gently,
Steal our lives away from us,
Blot out the vision of lost love,
Lost days, and all our ancient hungers;
Great Transformer,
Heal us!

Oh, softly, softly,
The great dark horses of Sleep are galloping over the
    land.
The tides of Sleep are moving in the hearts of men,
They flow like rivers in the night,
They flow with glut and fullness of their dark un-
    fathomed strength
Into a million pockets of the land
And over the shores of the whole earth,

They flow with the full might
Of their advancing and inexorable flood
Across the continent of night,
Across the breadth and sweep of the immortal earth,
Until the hearts of all men living
Are relieved of their harsh weight,
The souls of all men
Who have ever drawn in the breath of anguish and of
    labor
Are healed, assuaged, and conquered
By the vast enchantments of dark, silent
All-engulfing Sleep.

Sleep falls like silence on the earth,
It fills the hearts of ninety million men,
It moves like magic in the mountains,
And walks like night and darkness
Across the plains and rivers of the earth,
Until low upon lowlands, and high upon hills,
Flows gently Sleep,
Smooth-sliding Sleep—
Oh, Sleep—Sleep—Sleep!

As It Had Always Been

Grey twilight
Filtered through the windows once again.

The train had reached the tunnel's mouth.
On both sides now
Were ancient walls of masonry,
Old storied buildings,
Dark as time
And ancient as man's memory.

The boy peered through the window,
Up as far as eyes could reach,
At all those tiers of life,
Those countless cells of life,
The windows, rooms, and faces
Of the everlasting and eternal city.

They leaned above him
In their ancient silence.
They returned his look.
He looked into their faces
And said nothing,
No word was spoken.
The people of the city
Leaned upon the sills of evening
And they looked at him.

They looked at him
Through the silent yet attentive curtains
Of all their ancient and historic laundries.
They looked at him through pendant sheets,

Through hanging underwear,
Through fabrics of a priceless and unknown tapestry.
And he knew
That all was now as it had always been,
As it would be tomorrow and forever.

Immortal Drunkenness

Immortal drunkenness!
What tribute can we ever pay,
What song can we ever sing,
What swelling praise can ever be sufficient
To express the joy, the gratefulness, and the love
Which we, who have known youth and hunger in
     America,
Have owed to alcohol?

We are so lost, so lonely, so forsaken, in America:
Immense and savage skies bend over us,
And we have no door.

But you, immortal drunkenness,
Came to us in our youth
When all our hearts were sick with hopelessness,
Our spirits maddened with unknown terrors,
And our heads bowed down with nameless shame.

You came to us victoriously,
To possess us, and to fill our lives with your wild music,
To make the goat-cry burst from our exultant throats,
To make us know that here upon the wilderness, the
    savage land,
That here beneath immense, inhuman skies of time,
In all the desolation of the cities,
The gray unceasing flood-tides of the manswarm,
Our youth would soar to fortune, fame and love,
Our spirits quicken with the power of mighty poetry,
Our work go on triumphantly to fulfilment
Until our lives prevailed.

What does it matter, then,
If since that time of your first coming,
Magic drunkenness,
Our head has grown bald, our young limbs heavy,
And if our flesh has lain
Battered, bleeding in the stews?

You came to us with music, poetry, and wild joy,
When we were twenty,
When we reeled home at night
Through the old moon-whitened streets of Boston
And heard our friend, our comrade, and our dead com-
    panion,
Shout through the silence of the moonwhite square:
"You are a poet and the world is yours."

And victory, joy,
Wild hope, and swelling certitude
And tenderness
Surged through the conduits of our blood
As we heard that drunken cry,
And triumph, glory, proud belief
Was resting like a chrysm around us
As we heard that cry,
And turned our eyes then
To the moon-drunk skies of Boston,
Knowing only that we were young,
And drunk,
And twenty,
And that the power of mighty poetry
Was within us,
And the glory of the great earth
Lay before us—
Because we were young and drunk and twenty,
And could never die!

Fountain

On the Square
The slackened fountain
Dropped a fat spire of freezing water
Into its thickening rim of ice.

In summer, a tall spire
Blown in blue sheets of spray.
When they turned it down,
It wilted—
That was like a fountain, too.

This Is Man

For what is man?

First, a child, soft-boned,
Unable to support itself on its rubbery legs,
Befouled with its excrement,
That howls and laughs by turns,
Cries for the moon
But hushes when it gets its mother's teat;
A sleeper, eater, guzzler,
Howler, laugher, idiot,
And a chewer of its toe;
A little tender thing
All blubbered with its spit,
A reacher into fires,
A beloved fool.

After that, a boy,
Hoarse and loud before his companions,
But afraid of the dark;
Will beat the weaker and avoid the stronger;

Worships strength and savagery,
Loves tales of war and murder, and violence done to
    others;
Joins gangs and hates to be alone;
Makes heroes out of soldiers, sailors,
Prize-fighters, football players,
Cowboys, gunmen, and detectives;
Would rather die than not out-try
And out-dare his companions,
Wants to beat them and always to win,
Shows his muscle
And demands that it be felt,
Boasts of his victories
And will never own defeat.

Then the youth:
Goes after girls, is foul behind their backs
Among the drugstore boys,
Hints at a hundred seductions,
But gets pimples on his face;
Begins to think about his clothes,
Becomes a fop, greases his hair,
Smokes cigarettes with a dissipated air,
Reads novels, and writes poetry on the sly.
He sees the world now
As a pair of legs and breasts;
He knows hate, love, and jealousy;
He is cowardly and foolish,

He cannot endure to be alone;
He lives in a crowd, thinks with the crowd,
Is afraid to be marked off from his fellows
By an eccentricity.
He joins clubs and is afraid of ridicule;
He is bored and unhappy
And wretched most of the time.
There is a great cavity in him,
He is dull.

Then the man:
He is busy,
He is full of plans and reasons,
He has work.
He gets children,
Buys and sells small packets of everlasting earth,
Intrigues against his rivals,
Is exultant when he cheats them.
He wastes his little three-score years and ten
In spendthrift and inglorious living;
From his cradle to his grave
He scarcely sees
The sun or moon or stars;
He is unconscious of the immortal sea and earth;
He talks of the future
And he wastes it as it comes.
If he is lucky, he saves money.
At the end, his fat purse buys him flunkeys

To carry him where his shanks no longer can;
He consumes rich food and golden wine
That his wretched stomach has no hunger for;
His weary and lifeless eyes
Look out upon the scenery of strange lands
For which in youth his heart was panting.
Then the slow death,
Prolonged by costly doctors;
And finally the graduate undertakers,
The perfumed carrion,
The suave ushers with palms outspread to leftwards,
The fast motor-hearses,
And the earth again.

This is man:
A writer of books, a putter-down of words,
A painter of pictures,
A maker of ten thousand philosophies.
He grows passionate over ideas,
He hurls scorn and mockery at another's work,
He finds the one way, the true way, for himself,
And calls all others false—
Yet in the billion books upon the shelves
There is not one that can tell him
How to draw a single fleeting breath
In peace and comfort.
He makes histories of the universe,
He directs the destiny of nations,

But he does not know his own history,
And he cannot direct his own destiny
With dignity or wisdom
For ten consecutive minutes.

This is man:
For the most part
A foul, wretched, abominable creature,
A packet of decay,
A bundle of degenerating tissues,
A creature that gets old and hairless
And has a foul breath,
A hater of his kind,
A cheater, a scorner,
A mocker, a reviler,
A thing that kills and murders in a mob
Or in the dark,
Loud and full of brag surrounded by his fellows,
But without the courage of a rat, alone.
He will cringe for a coin,
And show his snarling fangs behind the giver's back;
He will cheat for two sous,
And kill for forty dollars,
And weep copiously in court
To keep another scoundrel out of jail.

This is man,
Who will steal his friend's woman,

Feel the leg of his host's wife below the table-cloth,
Dump fortunes on his whores,
Bow down in worship before charlatans,
And let his poets die.

This is man,
Who swears he will live only
For beauty, for art, for the spirit,
But will live only
For fashion,
And will change his faith and his convictions
As soon as fashion changes.

This is man,
The great warrior with the flaccid gut,
The great romantic with the barren loins,
The eternal knave devouring the eternal fool,
The most glorious of all the animals,
Who uses his brain for the most part
To make himself a stench
In the nostrils of the Bull, the Fox,
The Dog, the Tiger, and the Goat.

Yes, this is man,
And it is impossible to say the worst of him,
For the record of his obscene existence,
His baseness, lust, cruelty, and treachery,
Is illimitable.

His life is also full of toil, tumult, and suffering.
His days are mainly composed
Of a million idiot repetitions—
In goings and comings along hot streets,
In sweatings and freezings,
In the senseless accumulation of fruitless tasks,
In decaying and being patched,
In grinding out his life
So that he may buy bad food,
In eating bad food
So that he may grind his life out
In distressful defecations.
He is the dweller in that ruined tenement
Who, from one moment's breathing to another,
Can hardly forget the bitter weight of his uneasy flesh,
The thousand diseases and distresses of his body,
The growing incubus of his corruption.

This is man,
Who, if he can remember ten golden moments of joy
    and happiness
Out of all his years,
Ten moments unmarked by care,
Unseamed by aches or itches,
Has power to lift himself with his expiring breath,
And say: "I have lived upon this earth
And known glory!"

This is man,
And one wonders why he wants to live at all.
A third of his life is lost and deadened under sleep;
Another third is given to a sterile labor;
A sixth is spent in all his goings and his comings,
In the moil and shuffle of the streets,
In thrusting, shoving, pawing.
How much of him is left, then,
For a vision of the tragic stars?
How much of him is left
To look upon the everlasting earth?
How much of him is left for glory
And the making of great songs?
A few snatched moments only
From the barren glut and suck of living.

Here, then, is man,
This moth of time,
This dupe of brevity and numbered hours,
This travesty of waste and sterile breath.

Yet if the gods could come here
To a desolate, deserted earth
Where only the ruin of man's cities remained,
Where only a few marks and carvings of his hand
Were legible upon his broken tablets,
Where only a wheel lay rusting in the desert sand,
A cry would burst out of their hearts

And they would say:
"He lived, and he was here!"

Behold his works:

He needed speech to ask for bread—and he had Christ!
He needed songs to sing in battle—and he had Homer!
He needed words to curse his enemies—
And he had Dante, he had Voltaire, he had Swift!
He needed cloth to cover up his hairless, puny flesh
    against the seasons—
And he wove the robes of Solomon,
He made the garments of great kings,
He made the samite for the young knights!
He needed walls and a roof to shelter him—
And he made Blois!
He needed a temple to propitiate his God—
And he made Chartres and Fountains Abbey!
He was born to creep upon the earth—
And he made great wheels,
He sent great engines thundering down the rails,
He launched great wings into the air,
He put great ships upon the angry sea!

Plagues wasted him,
And cruel wars destroyed his strongest sons,
But fire, flood, and famine could not quench him.
No, nor the inexorable grave—

His sons leaped shouting from his dying loins.
The shaggy bison with his thews of thunder
Died upon the plains;
The fabled mammoths of the unrecorded ages
Are vast scaffoldings of dry insensate loam;
The panthers have learned caution
And move carefully among tall grasses to the water-
    hole;
And man lives on
Amid the senseless nihilism of the universe.

For there is one belief, one faith,
That is man's glory, his triumph, his immortality—
And that is his belief in life.
Man loves life,
And loving life, hates death,
And because of this he is great, he is glorious,
He is beautiful, and his beauty is everlasting.
He lives below the senseless stars
And writes his meanings in them.
He lives in fear, in toil,
In agony, and in unending tumult,
But if the blood foamed bubbling from his wounded
    lungs
At every breath he drew,
He would still love life more dearly
Than an end of breathing.
Dying, his eyes burn beautifully,

And the old hunger shines more fiercely in them—
He has endured all the hard and purposeless suffering,
And still he wants to live.

Thus it is impossible to scorn this creature.
For out of his strong belief in life,
This puny man made love.
At his best,
He *is* love.
Without him
There can be no love,
No hunger, no desire.

So this is man—the worst and best of him—
This frail and petty thing
Who lives his day
And dies like all the other animals,
And is forgotten.
And yet, he is immortal, too.
For both the good and evil that he does
Live after him.
Why, then, should any living man
Ally himself with death,
And, in his greed and blindness,
Batten on his brother's blood?

Ben, My Ghost

O sudden and impalpable faun,
Lost in the thickets of myself,
I will hunt you down
Until you cease to haunt my eyes with hunger.
I heard your foot-falls in the desert,
I saw your shadow in old buried cities,
I heard your laughter running down a million streets,
But I did not find you there.

And no leaf hangs for me in the forest;
I shall lift no stone upon the hills;
I shall find no door in any city.

But in the city of myself,
Upon the continent of my soul,
I shall find the forgotten language,
The lost world,
A door where I may enter,
And music strange as any ever sounded;

I shall haunt you, ghost,
Along the labyrinthine ways
Until—until?
O Ben, my Ghost,
An answer?

Full with the Pulse of Time

The river is a tide of moving waters:
By night it floods the pockets of the earth.
By night it drinks strange time, dark time.
By night the river drinks proud potent tides
Of strange dark time.
By night the river drains the tides,
Proud potent tides of time's dark waters
That, with champ and lift of teeth,
With lapse and reluctation of their breath,
Fill with a kissing glut the pockets of the earth.
Sired by the horses of the sea,
Maned with the dark,
They come.

They come! Ships call!
The hooves of night, the horses of the sea,
Come on below their manes of darkness.
And forever the river runs.
Deep as the tides of time and memory,
Deep as the tides of sleep,
The river runs.

And there are ships there!
Have we not heard the ships there?
(Have we not heard the great ships going down the
    river?

Have we not heard the great ships putting out to sea?)

Great whistles blow there.
Have we not heard the whistles blow there?
Have we not heard the whistles blowing in the river?
(A harness of bright ships is on the water.
A thunder of faint hooves is on the land.)

And there is time there.
(Have we not heard strange time, dark time,
Strange tragic time there?
Have we not heard dark time, strange time,
The dark, the moving tide of time
As it flows down the river?)

And in the night-time, in the dark there,
In all the sleeping silence of the earth,
Have we not heard the river, the rich immortal river,
Full of its strange dark time?

Full with the pulse of time it flows there,
Full with the pulse of all men living, sleeping,
Dying, waking,
It will flow there,
Full with the billion dark and secret moments of our
     lives
It flows there.
Filled with all the hope, the madness

And the passion of our youth
It flows there,
In the daytime, in the dark,
Drinking with ceaseless glut the land,
Mining into its tides the earth
As it mines the hours and moments of our life into its
    tides,
Moving against the sides of ships,
Foaming about piled crustings of old wharves,
Sliding like time and silence by the vast cliff of the city,
Girdling the stony isle of life with moving waters—
Thick with the wastes of earth,
Dark with our stains, and heavied with our dumpings,
Rich, rank, beautiful, and unending
As all life, all living,
As it flows by us, by us, by us,
To the sea!

The Bridge

What bridge?
Great God, the only bridge,
The bridge of power, life and joy,
The bridge that was a span, a cry, an ecstasy—
That was America.

What bridge?
The bridge whose wing-like sweep

Like space and joy and ecstasy
Was mixed like music in his blood,
Would beat like flight and joy and triumph
Through the conduits of his life forever.

What bridge?
The bridge whereon at night he had walked
And stood and watched, a thousand times,
Until every fabric of its soaring web
Was inwrought in his memory,
And every living sinew of its million cabled nerves
Had throbbed and pulsed in his own spirit
Like his soul's anatomy.

"The—the Brooklyn Bridge," he mumbled.
"The—the Bridge is good."

That Sharp Knife

Yes,
And in that month when Proserpine comes back,
And Ceres' dead heart rekindles,
When all the woods
Are a tender smoky blur,
And birds no bigger than a budding leaf
Dart through the singing trees,
And when odorous tar comes spongy in the streets,
And boys roll balls of it upon their tongues,

And they are lumpy with tops and agate marbles;
And there is blasting thunder in the night,
And the soaking million-footed rain,
And one looks out at morning on a stormy sky,
A broken wrack of cloud;
And when the mountain boy brings water
To his kinsmen laying fence,
And as the wind snakes through the grasses
Hears far in the valley below
The long wail of the whistle,
And the faint clangor of a bell;
And the blue great cup of the hills
Seems closer, nearer,
For he has heard an inarticulate promise:
He has been pierced by Spring,
That sharp knife.

And life unscales its rusty weathered pelt
And earth wells out in tender exhaustless strength,
And the cup of a man's heart runs over
With dateless expectancy, tongueless promise,
Indefinable desire.
Something gathers in the throat,
Something blinds him in the eyes,
And faint and valorous horns sound through the earth.

And little girls trot pigtailed
Primly on their dutiful way to school;

But the young gods loiter:
They hear the reed, the oaten-stop,
The running goathoofs in the spongy wood,
Here, there, everywhere;
They dawdle, listen,
Fleetest when they wait,
Go vaguely on to their one fixed home,
Because the earth is full of ancient rumor
And they cannot find the way.

All of the gods have lost the way.

Spring in the South

The harsh hill-earth
Has moistly thawed and softened,
Rich soaking rain falls,
Fresh-bladed tender grass
Like soft hair growing sparsely
Streaks the land.

By the cool orchards in the dark
The paper-carriers go.

The copper legs of negresses
In their dark dens stir.

The creek brawls cleanly.

New Orleans—River

And he looked upon
The huge yellow snake of the river,
Dreaming of its distant shores,
The myriad estuaries
Lush with tropical growth that fed it,
All the romantic life
Of plantation and canefields that fringed it,
Of moonlight,
Of dancing darkies on the levee,
Of slow lights on the gilded river-boat,
And the perfumed flesh of black-haired women,
Musical wraiths
Below the phantom drooping trees.

Come Back Again

Come up into the hills, O my young love.
Return! O lost and by the wind grieved ghost,
Come back again,
As first I knew you
In the timeless valley,
Where we shall feel ourselves anew,
Bedded on magic
In the month of June.

There was a place
Where all the sun went glistering
In your hair,
And from the hill
We could have put a finger
On a star.

Where is the day that melted
Into one rich noise?
Where the music of your flesh,
The rhyme of your teeth,
The dainty languor of your legs,
Your small firm arms,
Your slender fingers,
To be bitten like an apple—
And the little cherry-teats
Of your white breasts?
And where are all the tiny wires
Of finespun maidenhair?

Quick are the mouths of earth,
And quick the teeth
That fed upon this loveliness.
You who were made for music,
Will hear music no more:
In your dark house
The winds are silent.

Ghost, ghost, come back
From that marriage
That we did not foresee,
Return not into life
But into magic,
Where we have never died—
Into the enchanted wood,
Where we still lie,
Strewn on the grass.

Come up into the hills, O my young love:
Return.
O lost and by the wind grieved ghost,
Come back again.

The Locomotive

Then the locomotive drew in upon them,
Loomed enormously above them,
And slowly swept by them
With a terrific drive of eight-locked pistoned wheels,
All higher than their heads,
A savage furnace-flare of heat,
A hard hose-thick hiss of steam,
A moment's vision of a lean old head,
An old gloved hand of cunning on the throttle,
A glint of demon hawk-eyes fixed forever on the rails,

A huge tangle of gauges, levers, valves, and throttles,
And the goggled blackened face of the fireman,
Lit by an intermittent hell of flame,
As he bent and swayed with rhythmic swing of laden
    shovel
At his furnace doors.

The locomotive passed above them,
Darkening the sunlight from their faces,
Engulfing them at once
And filling them with terror,
Drawing the souls out through their mouths
With the God-head of its instant absoluteness,
And leaving them there,
Emptied, frightened, fixed forever,
A cluster of huddled figures,
A bough of small white staring faces,
Upturned, silent, and submissive,
Small, lonely, and afraid.

Then as the heavy rust-black coaches rumbled past,
And the wheels ground slowly to a halt,
The boy could see his mother's white stunned face
    beside him,
The naked startled innocence of her eyes,
And feel her rough worn clasp upon his arm,
And hear her startled voice,
Full of apprehension, terror, and surprise,

As she said sharply:
"Hah? What say? Is this his train?"

At Morning

At morning, in a foreign land,
Whether upon the mournful plains of Hungary,
Or in some quiet square of Georgian houses,
Embedded in the immensity of sleeping London,
He awakes, and thinks of home;
Or in some small provincial town of France,
He starts up from his sleep at night,
He starts up in the living, brooding stillness of the
    night,
For suddenly he thinks that he has heard there
The sounds of America and the wilderness,
The things that are in his blood, his heart, his brain,
In every atom of his flesh and tissue,
The things for which he draws his breath in labor,
The things that madden him
With an intolerable and nameless pain.

And what are they?
They are the whistle-wail
Of one of the great American engines
As it thunders through the continent at night,
The sound of the voices of the city streets—

Those hard, loud, slangy voices,
Full of violence, humor, and recklessness,
Now stronger and more remote than the sounds of
    Asia—
The sounds that come up
From the harbor of Manhattan in the night—
That magnificent and thrilling music
Of escape, mystery, and joy,
With the mighty orchestration of the transatlantics,
The hoarse little tugs, the ferryboats and lighters,
Those sounds that well up
From the gulf and dark immensity of night
And that pierce the entrails of the listener.

For this will always be
One of the immortal and living things about the land,
This will be an eternal and unchanging fact about that
    city
Whose only permanence is change:
There will always be the great rivers
Flowing around it in the darkness,
The rivers that have bounded so many nameless lives,
Those rivers which have moated in so many changes,
Which have girdled the wilderness
And so much hard, brilliant, and sensational living,
So much pain, beauty, ugliness,
So much lust, murder, corruption,
Love and wild exultancy.

They'll build great engines yet, and grander towers,
But always the rivers run,
In the day, in the night, in the dark,
Draining immensely their imperial tides out of the
    wilderness,
Washing and flowing by the coasts of the fabulous city,
By all the little ticking sounds of time,
By all the million lives and deaths of the city.

Always the rivers run,
And always there will be great ships upon the tide,
Always great horns are baying at the harbor's mouth,
And in the night a thousand men have died,
While the river, always the river,
The dark eternal river, full of strange secret time,
Washing the city's stains away,
Thickened and darkened by its dumpings,
Is flowing by us,
By us, to the sea.

He awakes at morning in a foreign land,
And he thinks of home.
He cannot rest,
His heart is wild with pain and loneliness,
He sleeps, but then he knows he sleeps,
He hears the dark and secret spell of time about him;
In ancient towns,
Thick tumbling chimes of the cathedral bells

Are thronging through the dark,
But through the passes of his diseased and unforgetful
    sleep
The sounds and memory of America make way:
Now it is almost dawn,
A horse has turned into a street
And, in America, there is the sound of wheels,
The lonely clop-clop of the hooves upon deserted pave-
    ments,
Silence,
Then the banging clatter of a can.

He awakes at morning in a foreign land,
He draws his breath in labor
In the wool-soft air of Europe:
The wool-gray air is all about him like a living sub-
    stance;
It is in his heart, his stomach, and his entrails;
It is in the slow and vital movements of the people;
It soaks down from the sodden skies into the earth,
Into the heavy buildings,
Into the limbs and hearts and brains of living men.
It soaks into the spirit of the wanderer;
His heart is dull with the gray weariness of despair,
It aches with hunger for the wilderness,
The howling of great winds,
The bite and sparkle of the clear, cold air,
The buzz, the tumult and the wild exultancy.

The wet, woolen air is all about him,
And there is no hope.

It was there before William the Conqueror;
It was there before Clovis and Charles "The Hammer";
It was there before Attila;
It was there before Hengist and Horsa;
It was there before Vercingetorix and Julius Agricola.

It was there now; it will always be there.
They had it in Merrie England and they had it in Gay
    Paree;
And they were seldom merry, and they were rarely gay.
The wet, woolen air is over Munich;
It is over Paris; it is over Rouen and Madame Bovary;
It soaks into England;
It gets into the boiled mutton and the Brussels sprouts;
It gets into Hammersmith on Sunday;
It broods over Bloomsbury
And the private hotels and the British Museum;
It soaks into the land of Europe and keeps the grass
    green.
It has always been there;
It will always be there.
His eyes are mad and dull;
He cannot sleep
Without the hauntings of phantasmal memory behind
    the eyes;

His brain is overstretched and weary,
It gropes ceaselessly around the prison of the skull,
It will not cease.

The years are walking in his brain,
His father's voice is sounding in his ears,
And in the pulses of his blood the tom-tom's beat.
His living dust is stored with memory:
Two hundred million men are walking in his bones;
He hears the howling of the wind around forgotten
      eaves;
He cannot sleep.
He walks in midnight corridors;
He sees the wilderness, the moon-drenched forests;
He comes to clearings in the moonlit stubble,
He is lost,
He has never been here,
Yet he is at home.
His sleep is haunted with the dreams of time;
Wires throb above him in the whiteness,
They make a humming in the noonday heat.

The rails are laid across eight hundred miles of golden
      wheat,
The rails are wound through mountains,
They curve through clay-yellow cuts,
They enter tunnels, they are built up across the marshes,
They hug the cliff and follow by the river's bank,

They cross the plains with dust and thunder,
And they leap through flatness and the dull scrub-pine
To meet the sea.

Then he awakes at morning in a foreign land,
And thinks of home.

Where Are We to Seek?

The years flow by like water,
And one day it is spring again.
Shall we ever ride out of the gates of the East again,
As we did once at morning,
And seek again, as we did then,
New lands, the promise of the war,
And glory, joy, and triumph,
And a shining city?

O youth, still wounded,
Living, feeling with a woe unutterable,
Still grieving with a grief intolerable,
Still thirsting with a thirst unquenchable—
Where are we to seek?

For the wild tempest breaks above us,
The wild fury beats about us,
The wild hunger feeds upon us—

And we are houseless, doorless, unassuaged,
And driven on forever;
And our brains are mad,
Our hearts are wild and wordless,
And we cannot speak.

Light of Fading Day

And the slant light steepened in the skies,
The old red light of waning day
Made magic fire upon the river,
And the train made on forever its tremendous monotone
That was like silence and forever—
And now there was nothing
But that tremendous monotone of time and silence
And the river, the haunted river,
The enchanted river
That drank forever its great soundless tides
From out the inland slowly,
And that moved through all men's lives
The magic thread of its huge haunting spell,
And that linked his life to magic kingdoms
And to lotus-land
And to all the vision of the magic earth
That he had dreamed of as a child,
And that bore him on forever
Out of magic

To all the grime and sweat and violence of the city,
And into America.

The great river burned there in his vision
In that light of fading day,
And it was hung there
In that spell of silence and forever,
And it was flowing on forever,
And it was stranger than a legend,
And as dark as time.

What Are We?

For what are we, my brother?
We are a phantom flare of grieved desire,
The ghostling and phosphoric flicker of immortal time,
A brevity of days haunted by the eternity of the earth.
We are an unspeakable utterance,
An insatiable hunger, an unquenchable thirst;
A lust that bursts our sinews, explodes our brains,
Sickens and rots our guts, and rips our hearts asunder.

We are a twist of passion,
A moment's flame of love and ecstasy,
A sinew of bright blood and agony,
A lost cry, a music of pain and joy,
A haunting of brief, sharp hours,

An almost captured beauty,
A demon's whisper of unbodied memory.
We are the dupes of time.

For, brother, what are we?

We are the sons of our father,
Whose face we have never seen,
We are the sons of our father,
Whose voice we have never heard,
We are the sons of our father,
To whom we have cried for strength and comfort
In our agony,
We are the sons of our father,
Whose life like ours
Was lived in solitude and in the wilderness,
We are the sons of our father,
To whom only can we speak out
The strange, dark burden of our heart and spirit,
We are the sons of our father,
And we shall follow the print of his foot forever.

The Great Ship

The great ship cast over them all her mighty spell:
Most of these people had made many voyages,
Yet the great ship caught them up again in her magic
    glow,

She possessed and thrilled them with her presence
As if they had been children.
The travellers stood there silent and intent
As the little boat slid in beside the big one,
They stood there with uplifted faces;
And for a moment it was strange and sad
To see them thus, with loneliness and longing in their
        eyes.
Their faces made small, lifted whitenesses;
They shone in the gathering dark with a luminous
        glimmer:
There was something small, naked and lonely
In the glimmer of those faces,
Around them was the immense eternity
Of sea and death.
They heard time.

For if, as men be dying,
They can pluck one moment from the darkness
Into which their sense is sinking,
If one moment in all the dark and mysterious forest
Should then live,
It might well be the memory of such a moment as this
Which, although lacking in logical meaning,
Burns for an instant in the dying memory
As a summary and symbol of man's destiny on earth.

The fading memory has forgotten

What was said then by the passengers,
The thousand tones and shadings of the living moment
Are forgotten,
But drenched in the strange, brown light of time,
The scene glows again for an instant
With an intent silence:
Darkness has fallen upon the eternal earth,
The great ship like a monstrous visitant
Blazes on the waters,
And on the tender the faces of the travellers
Are lifted up like flowers
In a kind of rapt and mournful ecstasy—
They are weary of travel,
They have wandered in strange cities
Among strange tongues and faces,
And they have left not even the print of their foot
In any town.

Their souls are naked and alone,
And they are strangers upon the earth,
And many of them long for a place
Where those weary of travel may find rest,
Where those who are tired of searching may cease to
    search,
Where there will be peace and quiet living,
And no desire.
Where shall the weary find peace:
Upon what shore will the wanderer come home at last?

When shall it cease—
The blind groping, the false desires, the fruitless am-
    bitions
That grow despicable as soon as they are reached,
The vain contest with phantoms,
The maddening and agony of the brain and spirit
In all the rush and glare of living,
The dusty tumult, the grinding, the shouting,
The idiot repetition of the streets,
The sterile abundance, the sick gluttony,
And the thirst which goes on drinking?

Out of one darkness
The travellers have come, to be taken into another,
But for a moment one sees their faces, awful and still,
All uplifted towards the ship.

This is all:
Their words have vanished,
All memory of the movements they made then
Has also vanished:
One remembers only their silence and their still faces
Lifted in the phantasmal light of lost time;
One sees them ever, still and silent,
As they slide from darkness on the river of time;
One sees them waiting at the ship's great side,
All silent and all damned to die,
With their grave, white faces

Lifted in a single supplication to the ship
And towards the silent row of passengers along the deck,
Who for a moment return their gaze
With the same grave and tranquil stare.

That silent meeting is a summary
Of all the meetings of men's lives:
In the silence
One hears the slow, sad breathing of humanity,
One knows the human destiny.

April

A light wind of April fanned over the hill.
There was a smell of burning leaves and rubble
Around the school.
In the field
On the hill flank behind the house
A plowman drove his big horse
With loose clanking traces
Around a lessening square of dry fallow earth.
Gee, woa.
His strong feet followed after.
The big share bit cleanly down,
Cleaving a deep spermy furrow of moist young earth
Along its track.

The Blazing Certitude

He turned, and saw her then,
And so finding her, was lost,
And so losing self, was found,
And so seeing her, saw for a fading moment only
The pleasant image of the woman that perhaps she **was,**
And that life saw.
He never knew:
He only knew that from that moment
His spirit was impaled upon the knife of love.

From that moment on
He never was again to lose her utterly,
Never to wholly re-possess unto himself
The lonely, wild integrity of youth
Which had been his.
At that instant of their meeting,
That proud inviolability of youth was broken,
Not to be restored.
At that moment of their meeting
She got into his life by some dark magic,
And before he knew it,
He had her beating in the pulses of his blood—
Somehow thereafter—how he never knew—
To steal into the conduits of his heart,
And to inhabit the lone, inviolable tenement of his **one**
    life;

So, like love's great thief,
To steal through all the adyts of his soul,
And to become a part of all he did and said and was—
Through this invasion
So to touch all loveliness that he might touch,
Through this strange and subtle stealth of love
Henceforth to share all that he might feel or make or
     dream,
Until there was for him no beauty that she did not share,
No music that did not have her being in it,
No horror, madness, hatred,
Sickness of the soul, or grief unutterable,
That was not somehow consonant
To her single image and her million forms—
And no final freedom and release,
Bought through the incalculable expenditure
Of blood and anguish and despair,
That would not bear upon its brow forever the deep
     scar,
Upon its sinews the old mangling chains,
Of love.

After all the blind, tormented wanderings of youth,
That woman would become his heart's centre
And the target of his life,
The image of immortal one-ness
That again collected him to one,
And hurled the whole collected passion, power and
     might

Of his one life
Into the blazing certitude,
The immortal governance and unity,
Of love.

Stranger than a Dream

And time still passing . . . passing like a leaf . . .
Time passing, fading like a flower . . .
Time passing like a river flowing . . .
Time passing . . . and remembered suddenly,
Like the forgotten hoof and wheel. . . .

Time passing as men pass
Who never will come back again . . .
And leaving us, Great God,
With only this . . .
Knowing that this earth, this time, this life,
Are stranger than a dream.

The Old House

--They flee us,
Who beforetime did us seek,
With desolate pauses sounding between our chambers,
The old chapters of the night

That sag and creak
And pass and stir
And come again.
They flee us, who beforetime did us seek.
And now, in an old house of life,
Forever in the dark mid-pause
And watches of the night,
We sit alone
And wait.

What things are these,
What shells and curios of outworn custom,
What relics here of old, forgotten time?
Festoons of gathered string and twines of thread,
And boxes filled with many buttons,
And bundles of old letters
Covered with scrawled and faded writings of the dead,
And on a warped old cupboard,
Shelved with broken and mended crockery,
An old wooden clock
Where Time his fatal, unperturbed measure keeps,
While through the night
The rats of time and silence
Gnaw the timbers of the old house of life.

A woman sits here
Among such things as these,
A woman old in years,

And binded to the past,
Remembering while storm shakes the house
And all the festoons of hung string sway gently
And the glasses rattle,
The way the dust rose on a certain day,
And the way the sun was shining,
And the sound of many voices that are dead,
And how sometimes in these mid-watches of the night
A word will come,
And how she hears a step
That comes and goes forever,
And old doors that sag and creak,
And something passing in the old house
Of life and time,
In which she waits
Alone.

Spring

Autumn was kind to them,
Winter was long to them—
But in April, late April,
All the gold sang.

Spring came that year like magic,
Like music, and like song.
One day its breath was in the air,
A haunting premonition of its spirit

Filled the hearts of men
With its transforming loveliness,
Working its sudden and incredible sorcery
Upon grey streets, grey pavements,
And on grey faceless tides of manswarm ciphers.

It came like music faint and far,
It came with triumph
And a sound of singing in the air,
With lutings of sweet bird-cries
At the break of day
And the high, swift passing of a wing,
And one day it was there
Upon the city streets
With a strange, sudden cry of green,
Its sharp knife of wordless joy and pain.

Not the whole glory
Of the great plantation of the earth
Could have outdone the glory of the city streets
That Spring.
Neither the cry of great, green fields,
Nor the song of the hills,
Nor the glory of young birch trees
Bursting into life again along the banks of rivers,
Nor the oceans of bloom in the flowering orchards,
The peach trees, the apple trees,
The plum and cherry trees—

Not all of the singing and the gold of Spring,
With April bursting from the earth
In a million shouts of triumph,
And the visible stride,
The flowered feet, of Springtime
As it came on across the earth,
Could have surpassed the wordless and poignant glory
Of a single tree in a city street
That Spring.

Like the First Day of the World

And he cried, "Glory! Glory!"
And we rode all through the night,
And round and round the park,
And then dawn came,
And all of the birds began to sing.

And now the bird-song broke in the first light,
And suddenly I heard each sound the bird-song made.
It came to me like music I had always heard,
It came to me like music I had always known,
The sounds of which I never yet had spoken,
And now I heard the music of each sound
As clear and bright as gold,
And the music of each sound was this:

At first it rose above me like a flight of shot,
And then I heard the sharp, fast skaps of sound the
  bird-song made.
And now they were smooth drops and nuggets of bright
  gold,
And now with chittering bicker and fast-fluttering skirrs
  of sound
The palmy, honied bird-cries came.
And now the bird-tree sang,
All filled with lutings in bright air;
The thrum, the lark's wing, and tongue-trilling chirrs
  arose.
And now the little brainless cries arose,
With liquorous, liquefied lutings,
With lirruping chirp, plumbellied smoothness, sweet
  lucidity.
And now I heard the rapid
Kweet-kweet-kweet-kweet-kweet of homely birds,
And then their pwee-pwee-pwee:
Others had thin metallic tongues,
A sharp cricketing stitch, and high shrews' caws,
With eery rasp, with harsh, far calls—
These were the sounds the bird-cries made.

All birds that are
Awoke in the park's woodland tangles;
And above them passed the whirr of hidden wings,
The strange lost cry of the unknown birds

In full light now in the park,
The sweet confusion of their cries was mingled.

"Sweet is the breath of morn,
Her rising sweet with charm of earliest birds,"
And it was just like that.
And the sun came up,
And it was like the first day of the world.

City April

Meanwhile the cat crept trembling at its merciless stride
Along the ridges of the backyard fences.
The young leaves turned and rustled in light winds of
    April,
And the sunlight came and went with all its sudden
    shifting hues
Into the pulsing heart of enchanted green.

The hoof and wheel went by upon the street,
As they had done forever,
The manswarm milled and threaded in the stupefaction
    of the streets,
And the high, immortal sound of time, murmurous and
    everlasting,
Brooded forever in the upper air
Above the fabulous walls and towers of the city.

The Ghosts of Time

Proud, cruel, everchanging and ephemeral city,
To whom we came once when our hearts were high,
Our blood passionate and hot,
Our brain a particle of fire:
Infinite and mutable city, mercurial city,
Strange citadel of million-visaged time—
O endless river and eternal rock,
In which the forms of life
Came, passed, and changed intolerably before us!
And to which we came, as every youth has come,
With such enormous madness,
And with so mad a hope—
For what?

To eat you, branch and root and tree;
To devour you,
Golden fruit of power and love and happiness;
To consume you to your sources,
River and spire and rock,
Down to your iron roots;
To entomb within our flesh forever
The huge substance of your billion-footed pavements,
The intolerable web and memory of dark million-
    visaged time.

And what is left now
Of all our madness, hunger, and desire?
What have you given,
Incredible mirage of all our million shining hopes,
To those who wanted to possess you wholly
To your ultimate designs, your final sources,
From whom you took the strength, the passion,
And the innocence of youth?

What have we taken from you,
Protean and phantasmal shape of time?
What have we remembered of your million images,
Of your billion weavings out of accident and number,
Of the mindless fury of your dateless days,
The brutal stupefaction of your thousand streets and
     pavements?
What have we seen and known that is ours forever?

Gigantic city, we have taken nothing—
Not even a handful of your trampled dust—
We have made no image on your iron breast
And left not even the print of a heel
Upon your stony-hearted pavements.
The possession of all things,
Even the air we breathed,
Was withheld from us,
And the river of life and time
Flowed through the grasp of our hands forever,

And we held nothing for our hunger and desire
Except the proud and trembling moments,
One by one.

Over the trodden and forgotten words,
The rust and dusty burials of yesterday,
We were born again into a thousand lives and deaths,
And we were left forever
With only the substance of our waning flesh
And the hauntings of an accidental memory,
With all its various freight of great and little things
Which passed and vanished instantly
And could never be forgotten,
And of those unbidden and unfathomed wisps and
    fumes of memory
That share the mind with all the proud dark images
Of love and death.

The tugging or a leaf upon a bough in late October,
A skirl of blown papers in the street,
A cloud that came and went
And made its shadow in the lights of April,
And the forgotten laughter of lost people in dark streets,
A face that passed us in another train,
The house our mistress lived in as a child,
A whipping of flame at a slum's cold corner,
The corded veins on an old man's hand,
The feathery green of a tree,

A daybreak in a city street in the month of May,
A voice that cried out sharply and was silent in the
    night,
And a song that a woman sang,
A word that she spoke at dusk before she went away—
The memory of a ruined wall,
The ancient empty visage of a half-demolished house
In which love lay,
The mark of a young man's fist in crumbling plaster,
A lost relic, brief and temporal,
In all the everlasting variousness of your life,
As the madness, pain and anguish
In the heart that caused it—
These are all that we have taken from you,
Iron-breasted city.
And they are ours and gone forever from us,
Even as things are lost and broken in the wind,
And as the ghosts of time are lost,
And as the everlasting river
That flowed past us in darkness to the sea.

Chance

Beyond all misuse, waste, pain, tragedy,
Death, confusion,
Unswerving necessity was on the rails;
Not a sparrow fell through the air

But that its repercussion
Acted on his life,
And the lonely light that fell
Upon the viscous and interminable seas
At dawn
Awoke sea-changes washing life to him.
The fish swam upward from the depth.

The seed of our destruction
Will blossom in the desert,
The alexin of our cure
Grows by a mountain rock,
And our lives are haunted
By a Georgia slattern
Because a London cut-purse went unhung.

Through Chance,
We are each a ghost to all the others,
And our only reality;
Through Chance,
The huge hinge of the world,
And a grain of dust;
The stone that starts an avalanche,
The pebble whose concentric circles
Widen across the seas.

You Were Not Absent

. . . of wandering forever and the earth again
. . . of seed-time, bloom, and the mellow-dropping
    harvest.
And of the big flowers, the rich flowers,
The strange unknown flowers.

Where shall the weary rest?
When shall the lonely of heart come home?
What doors are open for the wanderer?
And which of us shall find his father, know his face,
And in what place, and in what time,
And in what land?
Where?

Where the weary of heart can abide forever,
Where the weary of wandering can find peace,
Where the tumult, the fever, and the fret
Shall be forever stilled.

Who owns the earth?
Did we want the earth
That we should wander on it?
Did we need the earth
That we were never still upon it?
Whoever needs the earth shall have the earth:

He shall be still upon it,
He shall rest within a little place,
He shall dwell in one small room forever.

Did he feel the need of a thousand tongues
That he sought thus
Through the moil and horror of a thousand furious
    streets?
He shall need a tongue no longer,
He shall need no tongue for silence and the earth:
He shall speak no word through the rooted lips,
The snake's cold eye will peer for him
Through sockets of the brain,
There will be no cry out of the heart where wells the
    vine.

The tarantula is crawling through the rotted oak,
The adder lisps against the breast, cups fall:
But the earth will endure forever.
The flower of love is living in the wilderness,
And the elmroot threads the bones of buried lovers.

The dead tongue withers and the dead heart rots,
Blind mouths crawl tunnels through the buried flesh,
But the earth will endure forever;
Hair grows like April on the buried breast,
And from the sockets of the brain
The death-flowers grow and will not perish.

O flower of love
Whose strong lips drink us downward into death,
In all things far and fleeting,
Enchantress of our twenty thousand days,
The brain will madden
And the heart be twisted, broken by her kiss,
But glory, glory, glory, she remains:
Immortal love,
Alone and aching in the wilderness,
We cried to you:
You were not absent from our loneliness.

Old Men and Women

For them the past was dead:
They poured into our hands
A handful of dry dust and ashes.

The dry bones, the bitter dust?
The living wilderness, the silent waste?
The barren land?

Have no lips trembled in the wilderness?
No eyes sought seaward from the rock's sharp edge
For men returning home?
Has no pulse beat more hot with love or hate
Upon the river's edge?

Or where the old wheel and rusted stock
Lie stogged in desert sand:
By the horsehead a woman's skull.
No love?

No lonely footfalls in a million streets,
No heart that beat its best and bloodiest cry out
Against the steel and stone,
No aching brain, caught in its iron ring,
Groping among the labyrinthine canyons?

Naught in that immense and lonely land
But incessant growth and ripeness and pollution,
The emptiness of forests and deserts,
The unhearted, harsh and metal jangle of a million
    tongues,
Crying the belly-cry for bread,
Or the great cat's snarl for meat and honey?

All, then, all?
Birth and the twenty thousand days of snarl and jangle—
And no love, no love?
Was no love crying in the wilderness?

It was not true.
The lovers lay below the lilac bush;
The laurel leaves were trembling in the wood.

To Keep Time With

What is this dream of time,
This strange and bitter miracle of living?
Is it the wind that drives the leaves
Down bare paths fleeing?
Is it the storm-wild flight of furious days,
The storm-swift passing of the million faces,
All lost, forgotten, vanished as a dream?
Is it the wind that howls above the earth,
Is it the wind that drives all things before its lash,
Is it the wind that drives all men like dead ghosts flee-
     ing?
Is it the one red leaf that strains there on the bough
And that forever will be fleeing?
All things are lost and broken in the wind:
The dry leaves scamper down the path before us,
In their swift-winged dance of death
The dead souls flee along before us,
Driven with rusty scuffle
Before the fury of the demented wind.
And October has come again,
Has come again.

What is this strange and bitter miracle of life?
Is it to feel, when furious day is done,
The evening hush,

The sorrow of lost, fading light,
Far sounds and broken cries,
And footsteps, voices, music,
And all lost—
And something murmurous, immense and mighty, in
    the air?

And we have walked the pavements of a little town
And known the passages of barren night,
And heard the wheel, the whistle and the tolling bell,
And lain in the darkness waiting,
Giving to silence the huge prayer of our intolerable
    desire.
And we have heard the sorrowful silence
Of the river in October—
And what is there to say?
October has come again, has come again,
And this world, this life, this time
Are stranger than a dream.

May it not be that some day from this dream of time,
This chronicle of smoke, this strange and bitter miracle
    of life
In which we are the moving and phantasmal figures,
We shall awake?
Knowing our father's voice upon the porch again,
The flowers, the grapevines,
The low rich moon of waning August, and the tolling
    bell—

And instantly to know we live,
That we have dreamed and have awakened,
And find then in our hands some object, like this,
Real and palpable,
Some gift out of the lost land and the unknown world,
As token that it was no dream—
That we have really been there?
And there is no more to say.

For now October has come back again,
The strange and lonely month comes back again,
And you will not return.

Up on the mountain, down in the valley,
Deep, deep, in the hill, Ben—
Cold, cold, cold.

"To keep time with!"

Plum-Tree

The plum-tree, black and brittle,
Rocks stiffly in winter wind.
Her million little twigs are frozen
In spears of ice.

But in the Spring, lithe and heavy,
She will bend under her great load

Of fruit and blossoms.
She will grow young again.

Red plums will ripen,
Will be shaken desperately upon the tiny stems.
They will fall bursted
On the loamy warm wet earth.

When the wind blows in the orchard
The air will be filled with dropping plums;
The night will be filled
With the sound of their dropping.

And a great tree of birds will sing,
Burgeoning, blossoming richly,
Filling the air also
With warm-throated, plum-dropping bird-notes.

Moonlight

Then the moon blazed down
Upon the vast desolation of American coasts,
And on all the glut and hiss of tides,
On all the surge and foaming slide
Of waters on lone beaches.
The moon blazed down on 18,000 miles of coast,
On the million sucks and scoops and hollows of the
    shore,

And on the great wink of the sea,
That ate the earth minutely and eternally.

The moon blazed down upon the wilderness,
It fell on sleeping woods,
It dripped through moving leaves,
It swarmed in weaving patterns on the earth,
And it filled the cat's still eye with blazing yellow.

The moon slept over mountains
And lay like silence in the desert,
And it carved the shadows of great rocks like time.
The moon was mixed with flowing rivers,
And it was buried in the heart of lakes,
And it trembled on the water like bright fish.

The moon steeped all the earth
In its living and unearthly substance,
It had a thousand visages,
It painted continental space with ghostly light;
And its light was proper to the nature
Of all things it touched:
It came in with the sea,
It flowed with the rivers,
And it was still and living
On clear spaces in the forest
Where no men watched.

And in woodland darkness great birds fluttered to their
    sleep—
In sleeping woodlands, strange and secret birds,
The teal, the nightjar, and the flying rail
Went to their sleep with flutterings
Dark as hearts of sleeping men.

In fronded beds and on the leaves of unfamiliar plants
Where the tarantula, the adder, and the asp
Had fed themselves asleep on their own poisons,
And on lush jungle depths
Where, green-golden, bitter red and glossy blue,
Proud tufted birds cried out with brainless scream,
The moonlight slept.

The moonlight slept above dark herds
Moving with slow grazings in the night,
It covered lonely little villages;
But most of all
It fell upon the unbroken undulation of the wilderness,
And it blazed on windows,
And moved across the face of sleeping men.

Sleep lay upon the wilderness,
It lay across the faces of the nations,
It lay like silence on the hearts of sleeping men;
And low upon lowlands, and high upon hills,
Flowed gently sleep,

Smooth-sliding sleep—
Sleep—sleep.

Flood in Altamont

It began to rain—
Rain incessant,
Spouting, torrential rain,
Fell among the reeking hills,
Leaving grass and foliage
Drowned upon the slopes,
Starting the liquid avalanche of earth
Upon a settlement,
Glutting lean rocky mountain-streams
To a foaming welter of yellow flood.

It mined the yellow banks away
With unheard droppings;
It caved in hillsides;
It drank the steep banked earth away
Below the rails,
Leaving them
Strung to their aerial ties
Across a gutted canyon.

Gant's Dream

Gant went on then, down the road,
And there was a nameless sorrow in him
That he could not understand,
And some of the brightness had gone out of the day.

When he got to the mill,
He turned left
Along the road that went down by Spangler's run,
Crossed by the bridge below
And turned from the road
Into the wood-path on the other side.

A child was standing in the path,
And turned and went on ahead of him.
In the wood, the sunlight
Made swarming moths of light across the path,
And through the leafy tangle of the trees:
The sunlight kept shifting and swarming
On the child's gold hair,
And all around him
Were the sudden noises of the wood,
The stir, the rustle, and the bullet thrum of wings,
The cool broken sound of hidden water.

The wood got denser, darker
As he went on

And, coming to a place
Where the path split away into two forks,
Gant stopped and, turning to the child,
Said, "Which one shall I take?"
And the child did not answer him.

But some one was there in the wood before him.
He heard footsteps on the path,
And he saw a footprint in the earth
And, turning, took the path
Where the footprint was,
And where it seemed he could hear some one walking.

And then, with the bridgeless instancy of dreams,
It seemed to him
That all the bright green-gold around him in the wood
Grew dark and sombre, the path grew darker,
And suddenly he was walking
In a strange and gloomy forest
Haunted by the brown and tragic light of dreams.
The forest shapes of great trees rose around him,
He could hear no bird-song now,
Even his own feet on the path were soundless,
But he always thought he heard the sound
Of some one walking in the wood before him.

He stopped and listened: the steps were muffled,
Softly thunderous,

They seemed so near he thought he must catch up
With the one he followed, in another second,
And then they seemed immensely far away,
Receding in the dark mystery of that gloomy wood.
And again he stopped and listened,
The footsteps faded, vanished,
He shouted, no one answered.
And suddenly he knew that he had taken the wrong
    path,
That he was lost.
And in his heart there was an immense and quiet sad-
    ness,
And the dark light of the enormous wood
Was all around him;
No birds sang.

Gold and Sapphires

The day was like gold and sapphires:
There was a swift flash and sparkle,
Intangible and multifarious,
Like sunlight on roughened water,
All over the land.

A rich warm wind was blowing,
Turning all the leaves back the same way,
And making mellow music

Through all the lute-strings
Of flower and grass and fruit.
The wind moaned,
Not with the mad fiend-voice
Of winter in harsh boughs,
But like a fruitful woman,
Deep-breasted, great,
Full of love and wisdom;
Like Demeter, unseen and hunting
Through the world.

A dog bayed faintly in the cove,
His howl spent and broken by the wind.
A cowbell tinkled gustily.
In the thick wood below them
The rich notes of birds fell from their throats
Straight down, like nuggets.
A woodpecker drummed on the dry unbarked bole
Of a blasted chestnut-tree.

The blue gulf of the sky
Was spread with light massy clouds:
They cruised like swift galleons,
Tacking across the hills before the wind,
And darkening the trees below
With their floating shadows.

The Proud Stars

It was sunset.
The sun's vast rim, blood-red,
Rested upon the western earth,
In a great field of murky pollen.
It sank beyond the western ranges.

The clear sweet air was washed
With gold and pearl.
The vast hills melted
Into purple solitudes:
They were like Canaan and rich grapes.

The motors of cove people
Toiled up around the horse-shoe of the road.
Dusk came.
The bright winking lights in the town
Went up.

Darkness melted over the town like dew:
It washed out all the day's distress,
The harsh confusions.
Low wailing sounds came faintly
Up from Niggertown.

And above him
The proud stars flashed into heaven:
There was one, so rich and low,
That he could have picked it,
If he had climbed the hill
Beyond the Jew's great house.
One, like a lamp, hung low
Above the heads of men returning home.
(O Hesperus, you bring us all good things.)
One had flashed out the light
That winked on him
The night that Ruth lay
At the feet of Boaz;
And one on Queen Isolt;
And one on Corinth and on Troy.

It was night,
Vast brooding night,
The mother of loneliness,
That washes our stains away.
He was washed in the great river
Of night,
In the Ganges tides of redemption.
His bitter wound was for the moment
Healed in him:
He turned his face
Upward to the proud and tender stars,

Which made him a god and a grain of dust,
The brother of eternal beauty
And the son of death—
Alone, alone.

The Magic and the Loss

Oh, the wonder, the magic and the loss!
His life was like a great wave
Breaking in the lonely sea;
His hungry shoulder found no barriers—
He smote his strength at nothing,
And was lost and scattered
Like a wrack of mist.
But he believed
That this supreme ecstasy
Which mastered him and made him drunken
Might some day fuse its enormous light
Into a single articulation.
He was Phaeton
With the terrible horses of the sun:
He believed that his life
Might pulse constantly
At its longest stroke,
Achieve an eternal summit.

Like the Light

And above all else,
The Hudson River was like the light—
Oh, more than anything it was the light,
The light, the tone, the texture of the magic light
In which he had seen the city as a child,
That made the Hudson River wonderful.

The light was golden,
Deep and full with all rich golden lights of harvest;
The light was golden like the flesh of women,
Lavish as their limbs,
True, depthless, tender as their glorious eyes,
Fine-spun and maddening as their hair,
As unutterable with desire as their fragrant nests of
        spicery,
Their deep melon-heavy breasts.

The light was golden
Like a golden morning light
That shines through ancient glass
Into a room of old dark brown.

The light was brown,
Dark lavish brown

Hued with rich lights of gold;
The light was rich brown shot with gold
Like the sultry and exultant fragrance of ground coffee;
The light was lavish brown
Like old stone houses
Gulched in morning on a city street,
Brown like exultant breakfast smells
That come from basement areas
In the brownstone houses where the rich men lived;

The light was blue,
Steep frontal blue,
Like morning underneath the frontal cliff of buildings;
The light was vertical cool blue, hazed with thin morn-
    ing mist;
The light was blue,
Cold flowing harbor blue of clean cool waters
Rimed brightly with a dancing morning gold,
Fresh, half-rotten with the musty river stench,
Blue with the blue-black of the morning gulch and
    canyon of the city,
Blue-black with cool morning shadow as the ferry,
Packed with its thousand small white staring faces
    turned one way,
Drove bluntly toward the rusty weathered slips.

The light was amber brown
In vast dark chambers shuttered from young light

Where in great walnut beds the glorious women
Stirred in sensual warmth their lavish limbs.

The light was brown-gold
Like ground coffee, like the merchants
And the walnut houses where they lived,
Brown-gold like old brick buildings
Grimed with money and the smell of trade,
Brown-gold like morning in great gleaming bars of
      smart mahogany,
The fresh wet beer-wash, lemon-rind, and the smell
      of angostura bitters.

Then full-golden in the evening in the theaters,
Shining with full golden warmth and body
On full golden figures of the women,
On fat, red plush,
And on rich, faded, slightly stale smell,
And on the gilt sheaves and cupids and the cornucopias,
On the fleshly, potent, softly-golden smell of all the
      people;
And in great restaurants the light was brighter gold,
But full and round like warm onyx columns,
Smooth warmly tinted marble,
Old wine in dark rounded age-encrusted bottles,
And the great blonde figures of naked women
On rose-clouded ceilings.

Then the light was full and rich,
Brown-golden like great fields in autumn;
It was full swelling golden light like mown fields,
Bronze-red picketed with fat rusty golden sheaves of
    corn,
And governed by huge barns of red
And the mellow winey fragrance of the apples.—
Yes, all of this had been the tone and texture of the
    lights
That qualified his vision of the city and the river
When he was a child.

Judge Bland

But he was stained with evil.
There was something genuinely old and corrupt
At the sources of his life and spirit.
It had got into his blood,
His bone, his flesh.
It was palpable in the touch
Of his thin, frail hand when he greeted you,
It was present in the deadly weariness
Of his tone of voice,
In the dead-white texture
Of his emaciated face,
In his lank and lusterless auburn hair,
And, most of all,

In his sunken mouth,
Around which there hovered constantly
The ghost of a smile.
It could only be called the ghost of a smile,
And yet, really, it was no smile at all.
It was, if anything, only a shadow
At the corners of the mouth.
When one looked closely,
It was gone.
But one knew
That it was always there—
Lewd, evil, mocking,
Horribly corrupt,
And suggesting a limitless vitality
Akin to the humor of death,
Which welled up from some secret spring
In his dark soul.

Never Opened, Never Found

Smoke-gold by day,
The numb exultant secrecies of fog,
A fog-numb air filled with the solemn joy
Of nameless and impending prophecy,
An ancient yellow light,
The old smoke-ochre of the morning,

Never coming to an open brightness—
Such was October in England that year.

Sometimes by night in stormy skies
There was the wild, the driven moon,
Sometimes the naked time-far loneliness,
The most-oh-most familiar blazing of the stars
That shine on men forever,
Their nameless, passionate dilemma
Of strong joy and empty desolation,
Hope and terror, home and hunger,
The huge twin tyranny of their bitter governance—
Wandering forever and the earth again.

They are still-burning, homely particles of night,
That light the huge tent of the dark
With their remembered fire,
Recalling the familiar hill,
The native earth from which we came,
From which we could have laid our finger on them,
And making the great earth and home seem near,
Most near, to wanderers;
And filling them with naked desolations
Of doorless, houseless, timeless, and unmeasured va-
     cancy.

And everywhere that year
There was something secret, lonely, and immense

That waited, that impended, that was still.
Something that promised numbly, hugely,
In the fog-numb air,
And that never broke to any open sharpness,
And that was almost keen and frosty October
In remembered hills—
Oh, there was something there
Incredibly near and most familiar,
Only a word, a stride, a room, a door away—
Only a door away and never opened,
Only a door away and never found.

Some Things Will Never Change

In the window the man sat,
Always looking out.
He never wavered in his gaze,
His eyes were calm and sorrowful,
And on his face was legible
The exile of an imprisoned spirit.

That man's face became for me
The face of Darkness and of Time.
It never spoke,
And yet it had a voice—
A voice that seemed to have
The whole earth in it.

It was the voice of evening and of night,
And in it were the blended tongues
Of all those men
Who have passed through the heat and fury
Of the day,
And who now lean quietly
Upon the sills of evening.

In it was the whole vast hush and weariness
That comes upon the city at the hour of dusk,
When the chaos of another day is ended,
And when everything—
Streets, buildings,
And eight million people—
Breathe slowly,
With a tired and sorrowful joy.
And in that single tongueless voice
Was the knowledge
Of all their tongues.

"Child, child," it said,
"Have patience and belief,
For life is many days,
And each present hour will pass away.
Son, son,
You have been mad and drunken,
Furious and wild,
Filled with hatred and despair,

And all the dark confusions of the soul—
But so have we.
You found the earth too great
For your one life,
You found your brain and sinew
Smaller than the hunger and desire
That fed on them—
But it has been this way
With all men.
You have stumbled on in darkness,
You have been pulled in opposite directions,
You have faltered,
You have missed the way—
But, child,
This is the chronicle of the earth.

"And now,
Because you have known madness and despair,
And because you will grow desperate again
Before you come to evening,
We who have stormed the ramparts
Of the furious earth
And been hurled back,
We who have been maddened
By the unknowable and bitter mystery of love,
We who have hungered after fame
And savored all of life,
The tumult, pain, and frenzy,

And now sit quietly by our windows
Watching all that henceforth
Never more shall touch us—
We call upon you to take heart,
For we can swear to you
That these things pass.

"We have outlived
The shift and glitter of so many fashions,
We have seen
So many things that come and go,
So many words forgotten,
So many fames that flared
And were destroyed;
Yet we know now we are strangers
Whose footfalls have not left a print
Upon the endless streets of life.

"We shall not go into the dark again,
Nor suffer madness, nor admit despair:
We have built a wall about us now.
We shall not hear the clocks of time
Strike out on foreign air,
Nor wake at morning in some alien land
To think of home:
Our wandering is over, and our hunger fed.
O brother, son, and comrade,
Because we have lived so long

And seen so much,
We are content to make our own
A few things now,
Letting millions pass.

"Some things will never change.
Some things will always be the same.
Lean down your ear upon the earth,
And listen.

"The voice of forest water in the night,
A woman's laughter in the dark,
The clean, hard rattle of raked gravel,
The cricketing stitch of midday in hot meadows,
The delicate web of children's voices in bright air—
These things will never change.

"The glitter of sunlight on roughened water,
The glory of the stars,
The innocence of morning,
The smell of the sea in harbors,
The feathery blur and smoky buddings
Of young boughs,
And something there
That comes and goes
And never can be captured,
The thorn of spring,
The sharp and tongueless cry—

These things will always be the same.

"All things belonging to the earth will never change—
The leaf, the blade, the flower,
The wind that cries and sleeps and wakes again,
The trees, whose stiff arms
Clash and tremble in the dark,
And the dust of lovers
Long since buried in the earth—
All things proceeding from the earth to seasons,
All things that lapse and change
And come again upon the earth—
These things will always be the same,
For they come up from the earth that never changes,
They go back into the earth that lasts forever.
Only the earth endures,
But it endures forever.

"The tarantula, the adder, and the asp
Will also never change.
Pain and death will always be the same.
But under the pavements
Trembling like a pulse,
Under the buildings
Trembling like a cry,
Under the waste of time,
Under the hoof of the beast
Above the broken bones of cities,

There will be something growing
Like a flower,
Something bursting from the earth again,
Forever deathless, faithful,
Coming into life again
Like April."

Brooklyn

"Now is duh mont' of March, duh mont' of March—
Now it is Sunday afternoon in Brooklyn
In duh mont' of March,
An' we stand upon cold corners of duh day.
It's funny dat dere are so many corners
In duh mont' of March,
Here in Brooklyn where no corners are.
Jesus!

"On Sunday in duh mont' of March
We sleep late in duh mornin',
Den we get up an' read duh papers—
Duh funnies an' duh sportin' news.
We eat some chow.
An' den we dress up in duh afternoon,
We leave our wives,
We leave duh funnies littered on duh floor,
An' go outside in Brooklyn
In duh mont' of March

An' stand around upon ten t'ousand corners of duh day.
We need a corner in duh mont' of March,
A wall to stand to, a shelter an' a door.
Dere must be *some* place inside
In duh mont' of March,
But we never found it.
So we stand around on corners
Where duh sky is cold an' ragged still
Wit' winter,
In our good clothes we stand around
Wit' a lot of udder guys we know,
Before duh barber shop,
Just lookin' for a door."

Ah, yes, for in summer:

It is so cool and sweet tonight,
A million feet are walking here
Across the jungle web of Brooklyn
In the dark,
And it's so hard now
To remember
That it ever was the month of March
In Brooklyn
And that we couldn't find a door.

There are so many million doors tonight.
There's a door for everyone tonight,

All's open to the air,
All's interfused tonight:
Remote the thunder of the elevated trains on Fulton
     Street,
The rattling of the cars along Atlantic Avenue,
The glare of Coney Island seven miles away,
The mob, the racket, and the barkers shouting,
The cars swift-shuttling through the quiet streets,
The people swarming in the web,
Lit here and there with livid blurs of light,
The voices of the neighbors leaning at their windows,
Harsh, soft,
All interfused.

All's illusive in the liquid air tonight,
All mixed in with the radios
That blare from open windows.
And there is something over all tonight,
Something fused, remote, and trembling,
Made of all of this,
And yet not of it,
Upon the huge and weaving ocean of the night
In Brooklyn—
Something that we had almost quite forgotten
In the month of March.

What's this?—a sash raised gently?
A window?—a near voice on the air?

Something swift and passing,
Almost captured, there below?—
There in the gulf of night
The mournful and yet thrilling voices
Of the tugs?—the liner's blare?
Here—there—some otherwhere—
Was it a whisper?—a woman's call?
A sound of people talking
Behind the screens and doors
In Flatbush?

It trembles in the air
Throughout the giant web tonight,
As fleeting as a step—near--
As soft and sudden as a woman's laugh.
The liquid air is living
With the very whisper of the thing
That we are looking for tonight
Throughout America—
The very thing that seemed so bleak,
So cold, so hopeless, and so lost
As we waited in our good clothes
On ten thousand corners of the day
In Brooklyn
In the month of March.

The Song of the Whole Land

Smoke-blue by morning in the chasmed slant,
On, quickening the tempo of the rapid steps,
Up to the pinnacles of noon;
By day, and ceaseless,
The furious traffics of the thronging streets;
Forever now forevermore,
Upbuilding through the mounting flood-crest of these
    days,
Sky-hung against the crystal of the frail blue weather,
The slamming racketing of girdered steel,
The stunning riveting of the machines.
So soon the dark,
The sky-flung faery, and the great Medusa of the
    night;
'Twixt beetling seas, the star-flung crustaceans of the
    continent, and darkness—
Darkness, and the cool, enfolding night,
And stars and magic on America.

And across the plains the Overland, the continental
    thunders of the fast express,
The whistle-cry wailed back,
The fire-box walled and leveled on eight hundred miles
    of wheat;
The stiff rustling of the bladed corn at night in Indiana;
Down South, beside the road,

The country negro, clay-caked, marching, mournful,
And the car's brief glare;
The radiance of the mill at night,
The dynamic humming behind light-glazed glass,
Then the pines, the clay, the cotton fields again;
Fast-heard, soon-lost, the wheeling noises of the car-
    nival;
And sinners wailing from a church;
And then dumb ears beneath the river bed,
The voices in the tunnel stopped for Brooklyn;
But hackled moonlight on the Rocky Mountains,
Time-silence of the moon on painted rock;
In Tennessee, among the Knobs, down by the Holston
    River,
The last car coming by upon the road above,
Sounded horn and someone surely listening:

"That's those fellows. They've been to town.
They're coming in"—
And silence later and the Holston River;
But in Carlisle, a screen door slammed and voices going
And "Goodnight, goodnight, Ollie. Goodnight, May . . .
Where's Checkers? Did you let him out?"—
And silence, silence, and "Goodnight, goodnight";
The cop in Boston, twirling at the stick,
"Just one lone bum"—and ruminant—
"Just one lone bum upon the Common—that was all
    tonight;

Well, goodnight, Joe"—
The windows, fogged with pungent steam—
"Goodnight";
And moonlight on the painted buttes again—
"Meestaire . . . Oh-h, Meestaire"—
So eager, plaintive, pleading, strange—
And off the road, in the arroyo bed
A shattered Ford, a dead man, two drunk Mexicans—
"Meestaire"—and then
The eerie nearness of the wild coyote yelp—
"Meestaire"—and
It is seven miles to go to Santa Fe.

And the rustle of young leaves across America, and,
"Say it!" fierce, young, and low—
And fierce and panting, "Oh, I won't"—
Insistent, fierce, "You will! Now say it! Say it!"—
And the leaves softly, *'say it, say it'*—
And half-yielding, desperate, fierce, "Then . . . if you
    promise!"
The leaves, then, sighing, 'promise, promise'—
Quickly, fiercely, "Yes, I promise!"—
"I'll say it!"—
"Then say it! Say it!"—
And quickly, low, half-audible, " . . . Darling! . . .
    There! I said it!"—
Fierce, exultant, the boy's note, "Darling! Darling!
    Darling!"—

Wild and broken, "Oh, you promised!"—
Wild and fierce, "Oh, darling, darling, darling, darling,
    darling!"—
Despairing, lost, "You promised!"—
And the leaves, sadly, *'promised, promised, promised'*—
"Oh, darling, but you promised!"—
'Promised promised promised promised promised,'
Say the leaves across America.

And everywhere, through the immortal dark,
Something moving in the night,
And something stirring in the hearts of men,
And something crying in their wild, unuttered blood,
The wild, unuttered tongues of its huge prophecies—
So soon the morning,
Soon the morning:
O America.

The Ship

For men are wise:
They know that they are lost,
They know that they are desolate and damned together;
They look out upon the tumult of unending water,
And they know there is no answer,
And that the sea,
The sea, is its own end and answer.

Then they lay paths across it,
They make harbors at the end,
And log their courses to them,
They believe in earth and go to find it,
They launch great ships,
They put a purpose down upon the purposeless waste.

And this ship was the latest of them all
Upon the timeless seas.
She set a day, and fixed a mark on history.
She was the child of all other ships
That had made their dots of time
And that had brought small, vivid men and all their
      history
Upon the water—
The Greeks, and the Phœnician traders,
The wild, blond Norsemen with their plaited hair,
The hot Spaniards, the powdered Frenchmen with their
      wigs,
And the bluff English,
Moving in to close and board and conquer.

These men were lords and captains on tne sea,
And they had given mortal tongue, and
Meters of mortal time, to timelessness.
Yes! they made strong clocks
Strike sweetly out upon the ocean;
They took the timeless, yearless sea

And put the measure of their years upon it;
They said, "In such-and-such a year
We made this sea our own
And took her for our ship and country."

This was the ship,
And she was time and life there on the ocean.
If from sea-caves cold
The ageless monsters of the deep had risen,
The polyped squirm and women with no loins and sea-
    weed hair,
They could have read her time and destiny.
She cared for none of this,
For she was healthy with the life of man,
And men care little for the sea-cave cold.
In their few million years
What do they know
Of the vast swarming kingdoms of the sea,
Or of the earth
Beyond their scratchings on it?

Vision of the City

It was a cruel city, but it was a lovely one;
A savage city, yet it had such tenderness;
A bitter, harsh, and violent catacomb of stone and steel
    and tunneled rock,

Slashed savagely with light,
And roaring, fighting a constant ceaseless warfare of
    men and of machinery;
And yet it was so sweetly and so delicately pulsed,
As full of warmth, of passion, and of love,
As it was full of hate.

And even the very skies that framed New York,
The texture of the night itself,
Seemed to have the architecture and the weather
Of the city's special quality.

It was, he saw, a Northern city:
The bases of its form were vertical.
Even the night here, the quality of darkness,
Had a structural framework, and architecture of its own.
Here, compared with qualities of night
In London or in Paris,
Which were rounder, softer, of more drowsy hue,
The night was vertical, lean, immensely clifflike, steep
    and clear.
Here everything was sharp.
It burned so brightly, yet it burned sweetly, too.

For what was so incredible and so lovely
About this high, cool night
Was that it could be so harsh and clear,
So arrogantly formidable, and yet so tender, too.

There were always in these nights, somehow,
Even in nights of clear and bitter cold,
Not only the structure of lean steel,
But a touch of April, too:
They could be insolent and cruel,
And yet there was always in them
The suggestion of light feet, of lilac darkness,
Of something swift and fleeting,
Almost captured, ever gone,
A maiden virginal as April.

Here in this sky-hung faëry of the night,
The lights were sown like flung stars.
Suddenly he got a vision of the city
That was overwhelming in its loveliness.
It seemed to him all at once that there was nothing there
But the enchanted architecture of the dark,
Star-sown with a million lights.
He forgot the buildings:
All of a sudden, the buildings did not seem to exist,
To be there at all.
Darkness itself seemed to provide the structure
For the star-dust of those million lights,
They were flung there against the robe of night
Like jewels spangled on the gown of the dark Helen
That is burning in man's blood forevermore.

And the magic of it was incredible.

Light blazed before him, soared above him, mounted
    in linkless chains,
Was sown there upon a viewless wall, soared to the
    very pinnacles of night,
Inwrought into the robe of dark itself,
Unbodied, unsustained,
Yet fixed and moveless as a changeless masonry,
A world of darkness, the invisible,
Lighted for some immortal feast.

The Railroad Station

The station, as he entered it, was murmurous
With the immense and distant sound of time.
Great, slant beams of moted light
Fell ponderously athwart the station's floor,
And the calm voice of time
Hovered along the walls and ceiling
Of that mighty room,
Distilled out of the voices and movements
Of the people who swarmed beneath.

It had the murmur of a distant sea,
The languorous lapse and flow
Of waters on a beach.
It was elemental, detached,
Indifferent to the lives of men.

They contributed to it
As drops of rain contribute to a river
That draws its flood and movement
Majestically from great depths,
Out of purple hills at evening.

Few buildings are vast enough
To hold the sound of time,
And now it seemed to him
That there was a superb fitness in the fact
That the one which held it better than all others
Should be a railroad station.
For here, as nowhere else on earth,
Men were brought together for a moment
At the beginning or end
Of their innumerable journeys,
Here one saw their greetings and farewells,
Here, in a single instant,
One got the entire picture of the human destiny.
Men came and went, they passed and vanished,
And all were moving through the moments of their
    lives
To death,
All made small tickings in the sound of time—
But the voice of time remained aloof and unperturbed,
A drowsy and eternal murmur
Below the immense and distant roof.

Going Home Again

All through the night
He lay in his dark berth
And watched the old earth of Virginia
As it stroked past him
In the dream-haunted silence of the moon.
Field and hill and gulch
And stream and wood again,
The huge illimitable earth of America,
Kept stroking past him
In the steep silence of the moon.

All through the ghostly stillness of the land,
The train made on forever its tremendous noise,
Fused of a thousand sounds,
And they called back to him
Forgotten memories:
Old songs, old faces, old memories,
And all strange, wordless, and unspoken things
Men know and live and feel,
And never find a language for—
The legend of dark time,
The sad brevity of their days,
The unknowable but haunting miracle
Of life itself.

He heard again,
As he had heard throughout his childhood,
The pounding wheel, the tolling bell, the whistle-wail,
And he remembered how these sounds,
Coming to him from the river's edge
In the little town of his boyhood,
Had always evoked for him
Their tongueless prophecy
Of wild and secret joy,
Their glorious promises
Of new lands, morning, and a shining city.
But now the lonely cry of the great train
Was speaking to him,
With an equal strangeness, of return.
For he was going home again.

But why had he always felt so strongly
The magnetic pull of home,
Why had he thought so much about it
And remembered it with such blazing accuracy,
If it did not matter,
And if this little town
And the immortal hills around it
Were not the only home he had on earth?

He did not know.

All that he knew

Was that the years flow by like water,
And that one day
Men come home again.

The train rushed onward through the moonlit land.

October

October had come again,
And that year it was sharp and soon:
Frost was early,
Burning the thick green on the mountain sides
To massed brilliant hues of blazing colors,
Painting the air with sharpness,
Sorrow and delight—
And with October.

Sometimes, and often,
There was warmth by day,
An ancient drowsy light,
A golden warmth and pollenated haze in afternoon,
But over all the earth
There was the premonitory breath of frost,
An exultancy for all the men
Who were returning,
A haunting sorrow
For the buried men,

And for all those who were gone
And would not come again.

His father was dead,
And now it seemed to him
That he had never found him.
His father was dead,
And yet he sought him everywhere,
And could not believe that he was dead,
And was sure that he would find him.

It was October,
And that year,
After years of absence and of wandering,
He had come home again.

October is the richest of the seasons:
The fields are cut,
The granaries are full,
The bins are loaded to the brim with fatness,
And from the cider-press the rich brown oozings
Of the York Imperials run.

The bee bores to the belly of the yellowed grape,
The fly gets old and fat and blue,
He buzzes loud, crawls slow,
Creeps heavily to death
On sill and ceiling,

The sun goes down in blood and pollen
Across the bronzed and mown fields
Of old October.

The corn is shocked:
It sticks out in yellow rows
Upon dried ears,
Fit now for great red barns in Pennsylvania,
And the big stained teeth of crunching horses.
The indolent hooves kick swiftly at the boards,
The barn is sweet with hay and leather,
Wood and apples—
This, and the clean dry crunching of the teeth
Are all:
The sweat, the labor, and the plow
Are over.
The late pears mellow on a sunny shelf;
Smoked hams hang to the warped barn rafters;
The pantry shelves are loaded
With 300 jars of fruit.

Meanwhile, the leaves are turning, turning;
Up in Maine,
The chestnut burrs
Plop thickly to the earth
In gusts of wind,
And in Virginia
The chinkapins are falling.

There is a smell of burning
In small towns in afternoon,
And men with buckles on their arms
Are raking leaves in yards
As boys come by
With straps slung back across their shoulders.

The oak leaves, big and brown,
Are bedded deep in yard and gutter:
They make deep wadings to the knee
For children in the streets.
The fire will snap and crackle like a whip,
Sharp acrid smoke will sting the eyes,
In mown fields the little vipers of the flame
Eat past the black coarse edges of burned stubble
Like a line of locusts.
Fire drives a thorn of memory in the heart.

The bladed grass, a forest of small spears of ice,
Is thawed by noon:
Summer is over but the sun is warm again,
And there are days throughout the land
Of gold and russet.

But summer is dead and gone,
The earth is waiting,
Suspense and ecstasy

Are gnawing at the hearts of men,
The brooding prescience of frost is there.

The sun flames red and bloody as it sets,
There are old red glintings on the battered pails,
The great barn gets the ancient light
As the boy slops homeward with warm foaming milk.
Great shadows lengthen in the fields,
The old red light dies swiftly,
And the sunset barking of the hounds
Is faint and far and full of frost:
There are shrewd whistles to the dogs,
And frost and silence—
This is all.
Wind stirs and scuffs
And rattles up the old brown leaves,
And through the night
The great oak leaves keep falling.

Trains cross the continent
In a swirl of dust and thunder,
The leaves fly down the tracks behind them:
The great trains cleave through gulch and gulley,
They rumble with spoked thunder on the bridges
Over the powerful brown wash of mighty rivers,
They toil through hills,
They skirt the rough brown stubble of shorn fields,

They whip past empty stations in the little towns
And their great stride
Pounds its even pulse across America.

Field and hill
And lift and gulch and hollow,
Mountain and plain and river,
A wilderness with fallen trees across it,
A thicket of bedded brown and twisted undergrowth,
A plain, a desert, and a plantation,
A mighty landscape with no fenced niceness,
An immensity of fold and convolution
That can never be remembered,
That can never be forgotten,
That has never been described—
Weary with harvest,
Potent with every fruit and ore,
The immeasurable richness embrowned with autumn,
Rank, crude, unharnessed,
Careless of scars or beauty,
Everlasting and magnificent,
A cry, a space, an ecstasy!—

American earth in old October.

And the great winds howl and swoop across the land:
They make a distant roaring in great trees,
And boys in bed will stir in ecstasy,

Thinking of demons
And vast swoopings through the earth.
All through the night
There is the clean, the bitter rain
Of acorns,
And the chestnut burrs
Are plopping to the ground.

And often in the night
There is only the living silence,
The distant frosty barking of a dog,
The small clumsy stir and feathery stumble
Of the chickens on limed roosts,
And the moon,
The low and heavy moon of autumn,
Now barred behind the leafless poles of pines,
Now at the pine-woods' brooding edge and summit,
Now falling with ghost's dawn of milky light
Upon rimed clods of fields
And on the frosty scurf on pumpkins,
Now whiter, smaller, brighter,
Hanging against the steeple's slope,
Hanging the same way in a million streets,
Steeping all the earth
In frost and silence.

Then a chime of frost-cold bells
May peal out on the brooding air,

And people lying in their beds will listen.
They will not speak or stir,
Silence will gnaw the darkness like a rat,
But they will whisper in their hearts:
"Summer has come and gone,
Has come and gone.
And now—?"

But they will say no more,
They will have no more to say:
They will wait listening,
Silent and brooding as the frost,
To time, strange ticking time,
Dark time that haunts us
With the briefness of our days.
They will think of men long dead,
Of men now buried in the earth,
Of frost and silence long ago,
Of a forgotten face and moment of lost time,
And they will think of things they have no words to
    utter.

And in the night, in the dark,
In the living sleeping silence of the towns,
The million streets,
They will hear the thunder of the fast express,
The whistles of great ships upon the river.

What will they say then?
What will they say?

Come to us, Father, in the watches of the night,
Come to us as you always came,
Bringing to us
The invincible sustenance of your strength,
The limitless treasure of your bounty,
The tremendous structure of your life
That will shape all lost and broken things on earth
Again into a golden pattern of exultancy and joy.

Come to us, Father,
While the winds howl in the darkness,
For October has come again
Bringing with it huge prophecies of death and life
And the great cargo of the men who will return.
For we are ruined, lost, and broken
If you do not come,
And our lives, like rotten chips,
Are whirled about us
Onward in darkness
To the sea.

The Silence of the House

This is the house
In which I have been an exile.

There is a stranger in the house,
And there's a stranger in me.

O house of Admetus,
In whom (although I was a god)
I have endured so many things.
Now, house, I am not afraid.
No ghost need fear come by me.
If there's a door in silence,
Let it open.
My silence can be greater than your own.
And you who are in me,
And who I am,
Come forth beyond this quiet shell of flesh
That makes no posture to deny you.
There is none to look at us:
Oh come, my brother and my lord,
With unbent face.

If I had 40,000 years,
I should give all but the ninety last
To silence.
I should grow to the earth
Like a hill or a rock.
Unweave the fabric of nights and days;
Unwind my life back to my birth;
Subtract me into nakedness again,
And build me back with all the sums I have not counted.

Or let me look upon the living face of darkness;
Let me hear the terrible sentence of your voice.

There was nothing but the living silence of the house:
No doors were opened.

Time

I

"Long, long into the night I lay—"
(One!)
"Long, long into the night I lay awake—"
(Two!)
"Long, long into the night I lay awake,
Thinking how I should tell my story."

Oh how lovely those words are!
They make a music in me just like bells.

(*One*, Two, Three, Four!
One, *Two*, Three, Four!)

Oh there are bells, and that is time!
What time is that?
That was the half hour
That the bells were striking.
And that was time, time, time.

And that was time, dark time.
Yes, that was time, dark time,
That hangs above our heads in lovely bells.

Time.
You hang time up
In great bells in a tower,
You keep time ticking
In a delicate pulse upon your wrist,
You imprison time
Within the small, coiled wafer of a watch,
And each man has his own,
A separate time.

II

There, tell me; tell me, there:
Where is lost time now?
Where are lost ships, lost faces, and lost love?
Where is the lost child now?
Did no one see her o'er the tangled shipping?
Did no one see her by light waters?
Lost?
Did no one speak to her?
Ah, please, can no one find her, hold her, keep her—
Bring her back to me?
Gone?
Just for a moment, I beseech you,

Just for a moment out of measured, meted,
And unmindful time!

Gone?
Then is she lost?
Can no one bring me back a child?
You'll build great engines yet and taller towers,
Our dust will tremble to far greater wheels:
Have you no engines, then,
To bring back sixty seconds
Of lost time?

Then she is lost.

III

"Long, long into the night I lay awake,
Thinking how I should tell my story."

(One!)
Now in the dark I hear the boats
There in the river.
(Two!)
Now I can hear the great horns
Blowing in the river.

Time! Where are you now,
And in what place, and at what time?

Oh now I hear the whistles on the river!
Oh now great ships are going down the river!
Great horns are baying at the harbor's mouth,
Great boats are putting out to sea!

And in the nighttime, in the dark,
In all the sleeping silence of the earth,
The river, the dark rich river,
Full of strange time, dark time,
Strange tragic time,
Is flowing,
Flowing out to sea!

IV

"Long, long into the night I lay awake—"
(One!)
Come, mild sleep,
Seal up the porches of our memory . . .
(Two!)
Come, magnificent sleep,
Blot out the vision of lost days . . .
(Three!)
For we are strange and beautiful
Asleep,
We are all strange and beautiful
Asleep . . .
(Four!)

For we are dying in the darkness,
And we know no death,
There is no death in sleep. . . .

O daughter of unmemoried hours,
Empress of labor and of weariness,
Merciful sister of dark death
And all forgetfulness,
Enchantress and redeemer,
Hail!

V

Time is a fable and a mystery:
It has ten thousand visages,
It broods on all the images of earth,
And it transmutes them
With a strange, unearthly glow.

Time is collected in great clocks
And hung in towers,
The ponderous bells of time
Throng through the darkened air of sleeping cities,
Time beats its tiny pulse out
In small watches on a woman's wrist,
Time begins and ends the life of every man,
And each man has his own,
A different time.

Burning in the Night

Go, seeker, if you will, throughout the land
And you will find us burning in the night.

There where the hackles of the Rocky Mountains
Blaze in the blank and naked radiance of the moon,
Go—
Make your resting-stool upon the highest peak.
Can you not see us now?

The continental wall juts sheer and flat,
Its huge black shadow on the plain,
And the plain sweeps out against the East,
Two thousand miles away.
The great snake that you see there
Is the Mississippi River.

Behold
The gem-strung towns and cities
Of the good, green East,
Flung like star-dust through the field of night.
That spreading constellation to the north
Is called Chicago,
And that giant wink that blazes in the moon
Is the pendant lake that it is built upon.
Beyond, close-set and dense as a clenched fist,

Are all the jeweled cities of the eastern seaboard.
There's Boston,
Ringed with the bracelet of its shining little towns,
And all the lights that sparkle
On the rocky indentations of New England.
Here, southward and a little to the west,
And yet still coasted to the sea,
Is our intensest ray,
The splintered firmament of the towered island
Of Manhattan.
Round about her, sown thick as grain,
Is the glitter of a hundred towns and cities.
The long chain of lights there
Is the necklace of Long Island and the Jersey shore.
Southward and inland, by a foot or two,
Behold the duller glare of Philadelphia.
Southward further still,
The twin constellations—Baltimore and Washington.
Westward, but still within the borders
Of the good, green East,
That nighttime glow and smolder of hell-fire
Is Pittsburgh.
Here, St. Louis, hot and humid
In the cornfield belly of the land,
And bedded on the mid-length coil and fringes
Of the snake.
There at the snake's mouth,
Southward six hundred miles or so,

You see the jeweled crescent of old New Orleans.
Here, west and south again,
You see the gemmy glitter
Of the cities on the Texas border.

Turn now, seeker,
On your resting-stool atop the Rocky Mountains,
And look another thousand miles or so
Across moon-blazing fiend-worlds of the Painted Desert
And beyond Sierra's ridge.
That magic congeries of lights
There to the west,
Ringed like a studded belt
Around the magic setting of its lovely harbor,
Is the fabled town of San Francisco.
Below it, Los Angeles
And all the cities of the California shore.
A thousand miles to north and west,
The sparkling towns of Oregon and Washington.

Observe the whole of it,
Survey it as you might survey a field.
Make it your garden, seeker,
Or your backyard patch.
Be at ease in it.
It's your oyster—yours to open if you will.
Don't be frightened,
It's not so big now,

When your footstool is the Rocky Mountains.
Reach out
And dip a hatful of cold water
From Lake Michigan.
Drink it—we've tried it—
You'll not find it bad.
Take your shoes off
And work your toes down in the river oozes
Of the Mississippi bottom—
It's very refreshing
On a hot night in the summertime.

Help yourself to a bunch of Concord grapes
Up there in northern New York State—
They're getting good now.
Or raid that watermelon patch
Down there in Georgia.
Or, if you like, you can try the Rockyfords
Here at your elbow, in Colorado.
Just make yourself at home,
Refresh yourself, get the feel of things,
Adjust your sights, and get the scale.
It's your pasture now, and it's not so big—
Only three thousand miles from east to west,
Only two thousand miles from north to south—
But all between,
Where ten thousand points of light
Prick out the cities, towns, and villages,

There, seeker,
You will find us burning in the night.

Here, as you pass through the brutal sprawl,
The twenty miles of rails and rickets,
Of the South Chicago slums—
Here, in an unpainted shack, is a negro boy,
And, seeker,
He is burning in the night.
Behind him is a memory of the cotton fields,
The flat and mournful pineland barrens
Of the lost and buried South,
And at the fringes of the pine
Another nigger shack,
With mammy and eleven little niggers.
Farther still behind,
The slave-driver's whip, the slave ship,
And, far off,
The jungle dirge of Africa.
And before him, what?
A roped-in ring, a blaze of lights,
Across from him a white champion;
The bell, the opening,
And all around
The vast sea-roaring of the crowd.
Then the lightning feint and stroke,
The black panther's jaw—
The hot, rotating presses,

And the rivers of sheeted print!
O seeker, where is the slave ship now?

Or there,
In the clay-baked piedmont of the South,
That lean and tan-faced boy
Who sprawls there in the creaking chair
Among admiring cronies
Before the open doorways of the fire department,
And tells them how he pitched the team
To shut-out victory today.
What visions burn, what dreams possess him,
Seeker of the night?
The packed stands of the stadium,
The bleachers sweltering with their unshaded hordes,
The faultless velvet of the diamond,
Unlike the clay-baked outfields down in Georgia,
The mounting roar of eighty thousand voices
And Gehrig coming up to bat,
The boy himself upon the pitching mound,
The lean face steady as a hound's;
Then the nod, the signal, and the wind-up,
The rawhide arm that snaps and crackles like a whip,
The small white bullet of the blazing ball,
Its loud report in the oiled pocket of the catcher's mitt,
The umpire's thumb jerked upward,
The clean strike.

Or there again,
In the East-Side Ghetto of Manhattan,
Two blocks away from the East River,
A block away from the gas-house district and its thug-
    gery,
There in the swarming tenement,
Shut in his sweltering cell,
Breathing the sun-baked air
Through opened window at the fire-escape,
Celled there away
Into a little semblance of privacy and solitude
From all the brawling and vociferous life and argu-
    ment
Of his family and the seething hive around him,
The Jew boy sits and pores upon his book.
In shirt-sleeves, bent above his table
To meet the hard glare of a naked bulb,
He sits
With gaunt, starved face converging to his huge beaked
    nose,
The weak eyes squinting painfully
Through his thick-lens glasses,
His greasy hair roached back in oily scrolls
Above the slanting cage
Of his painful and constricted brow.
And for what?
For what this agony of concentration?

For what this hell of effort?
For what this intense withdrawal
From the poverty and squalor
Of dirty brick and rusty fire-escapes,
From the raucous cries and violence
And never-ending noise?
For what?
Because, brother,
He is burning in the night.
He sees the class, the lecture room,
The shining apparatus of gigantic laboratories,
The open field of scholarship and pure research,
Certain knowledge,
And the world distinction of an Einstein name.

So, then, to every man his chance—
To every man, regardless of his birth,
His shining, golden opportunity—
To every man the right to live,
To work, to be himself,
And to become
Whatever thing his manhood and his vision
Can combine to make him—
This, seeker,
Is the promise of America.

Toward Which

Something has spoken to me in the night,
Burning the tapers of the waning year;
Something has spoken in the night,
And told me I shall die, I know not where.

Saying:
"To lose the earth you know, for greater knowing;
To lose the life you have, for greater life;
To leave the friends you loved, for greater loving;
To find a land more kind than home, more large than
    earth—

"—Whereon the pillars of this earth are founded,
Toward which the conscience of the world is tending—
A wind is rising, and the rivers flow."